Grammar
Practice for
Intermediate
Students

Elaine Walker
Steve Elsworth

Grammar Practice for Intermediate Students

Longman

Longman Group UK Limited
Longman House, Burnt Mill, Harlow,
Essex CM20 2JE, England
and Associated Companies throughout the world.

First published 1986
Fifth impression 1988

Illustrated by David Mostyn

Set in 9/10pt 'Monophoto' Helvetica Light and Medium
Produced by Longman Group (FE) Ltd
Printed in Hong Kong

ISBN 0-582-55894-8

To the student

Grammar Practice for Intermediate Students gives short, clear explanations of all the main areas of English grammar, and provides practice exercises for you to do. The exercises are given one, two, or three stars:

★ = easy

★★ = more difficult

★★★ = the most difficult

There are two ways in which this book can be used:

(i) in class, with help from your teacher;
(ii) at home by yourself.

If you are using the book by yourself, use the Index and the Contents list to find the areas that you want to study, read the grammatical explanation, and then do the exercise. You can check your answers in *Grammar Practice for Intermediate Students Key*, which is published separately.

We hope that *Grammar Practice for Intermediate Students* helps you to improve your English.

Elaine Walker
Steve Elsworth

Contents

Nouns, adjectives, and adverbs

Nouns, pronouns, and articles

1 ★
Subject and object pronouns

Subject pronouns

I	you	he	she	it	we	you	they

Object pronouns

me	you	him	her	it	us	you	them

- The subject is the person or thing doing the action:
  I left early.
  She went home.
  We said goodbye.

- The object is the person or thing receiving the action:
  She telephoned me.
  I hit him.
  We saw her.

I left early.

Write the correct *pronouns* for these sentences:

1 . . . . telephoned yesterday. (she)
   She telephoned yesterday.
2 We watch . . . . for hours. (he)
   We watched him for hours.
3 Hasn't . . . . arrived yet? (she)
4 . . . . don't understand. (I)
5 Are you talking to . . . .? (I)
6 Don't ask . . . .: . . . . doesn't know. (she/she)
7 This is Julia: . . . . have known . . . . for years. (we/she)
8 Nobody told . . . . the bus was leaving. (they)
9 Why didn't . . . . ask . . . . to come? (she/they)
10 Don't ask . . . .: ask . . . . . (I/he)
11 . . . . think . . . . doesn't like . . . . . (I/he/I)
12 . . . . asked . . . . to invite . . . . . (they/he/we)

2   ⋆
Possessive adjectives

● Each pronoun has a possessive adjective:

I	→ my	we	→ our
you	→ your	you	→ your
he	→ his	they	→ their
she	→ her	it	→ its

Write the correct *adjectives* for these sentences:

1   These are . . . . parents. (I)
     These are my parents.
2   I've got . . . . watch. (he)
3   Is this . . . . car? (you)
4   Do they like . . . . new house? (she)
5   Have you met . . . . teacher? (they)
6   Who's got . . . . money? (I)
7   I don't like . . . . teacher. (we)
8   Have you got . . . . passport? (you)
9   He forgot . . . . keys. (he)
10   They changed . . . . hotel. (they)
11   She gave the letter to . . . . secretary. (she)
12   There's something wrong with . . . . car. (I)
13   They're having a party in . . . . garden. (they)
14   Where's . . . . pen? (I)
15   I like . . . . jacket. (you)

3   ⋆
Possessive adjectives and pronouns

Possessive adjectives

my	your	his	her	its	our	your	their

Possessive pronouns

mine	yours	his	hers	—	ours	yours	theirs

● The possessive adjective is always followed by its noun:
     *It's **my** car.*
     *That's **his** mother.*
     *This is **our** house.*

● The possessive pronoun is never followed by its noun:
     *This is **mine**.*
     *Give it to Peter: it's **his**.*
     *The money is **ours**.*

Write the correct *adjective* or *pronoun* for these sentences:

1   Whose camera is this? Is it . . . .? (you)
    Whose camera is this? Is it yours?
2   Excuse me, those are . . . . seats. (we)
    Excuse me, those are our seats.
3   Is it . . . . suitcase or . . . .? (you/he)
    Is it your suitcase or his?
4   Has the dog had . . . . food? (it)
5   They're not . . . . keys – they're . . . . . (I/she)
6   I don't think it's . . . . room: I think it's . . . . . (you/they)
7   The police asked me for . . . . address. (I)
8   Have you got . . . . pen, or would you like to borrow . . . .? (you/I)
9   . . . . garden is bigger than . . . . . (they/we)
10 I think this is . . . . book. Oh no, it's . . . . . (I/you)
11 The decision is . . . . . (they)
12 The cat wants . . . . dinner. (it)
13 You know it's not . . . . money. It's . . . . . (you/I)
14 It isn't . . . . car, it's . . . . . (he/she)
15 It wasn't . . . . mistake, it was . . . . . (I/they)
16 Have you met . . . . mother? (they)
17 . . . . parents say the garden is . . . . . (she/they)
18 . . . . brother thinks the car is . . . . . (I/we)
19 . . . . car wasn't working, so I used . . . . . (I/he)
20 . . . . house is smaller than . . . . . (we/they)

4   ★
The possessive with 's

●   To indicate possession for people or animals:
    a) in the singular, add **'s**:
       Anne's bike.
       James's friend.
       The dog's food.

    b) for plurals ending in **-s**, just add **'**:
       The boys' mother.
       My parents' house.
       The ladies' hats.

    c) for other plurals, add **'s**:
       The children's friends.
       The women's cars.

*   Note: **it's** = **it is**. The possessive of **it** is **its**:
    It's cold today.
    Give the dog its food.

It's cold today.

Rewrite these sentences, putting the apostrophe (') where necessary. If two answers are possible, write the more likely one:

1   We talked to the boys parents for some time.
     We talked to the boys' parents for some time.
     We talked to the boy's parents for some time.
2   We can borrow my fathers car.
     We can borrow my father's car.
3   Have you met Susans friend?
4   About sixty people use the teachers room.
5   Someone has taken Barbaras purse.
6   Something was hurting the animals foot.
7   I'm going to write to the childrens parents.
8   Jane works in my mothers office.
9   The dog doesn't like its food.
10   Mary and Pat stayed at their friends house.
11   Are you going to the secretaries meeting?
12   I put the money in the waiters hand.
13   Ians suit was very expensive.
14   What did you think of the new students party?
15   The policemans car was not damaged.
16   The dog was looking for its ball.
17   Ann won the Womens Championship last year.

5   ★★
Other possessives

●   To indicate possession for things:
     a) use **of**:
        *The end **of** the road.*
        *The smell **of** cooking.*
        *The leader **of** the party.*

     b) for common nouns (*house, car, school, table*, etc) **of** is not
        necessary, and the word position changes:
        Car keys.
        The kitchen door.
        A bus driver.

     c) for expressions of time **'s** is used:
        *A fortnight**'s** holiday.*
        *Two week**s'** rest.*

Use the correct possessives to complete the sentences. If two answers are possible, write the more likely one:

1   I opened the . . . . . (door/car)
     I opened the car door.
2   My keys are in the . . . . . (pocket/my suit)
     My keys are in the pocket of my suit.
3   I opened the . . . . . (door/kitchen)

4   She put her suitcase in the . . . . . (car/boot)
5   My room is at the . . . . . (front/hotel)
6   We sat on the . . . . . (carpet/sitting-room)
7   I'm afraid I've broken the . . . . . (leg/chair)
8   Would you turn on the . . . . .? (light/kitchen)
9   Someone has damaged the . . . . . (front/my car)
10 This is Mrs Davies, the . . . . . (manager/cinema)
11 The cat walked along the . . . . . (wall/garden)
12 Would someone open the . . . .? (window/bathroom)
13 The doctor told me to have a . . . . . (week/rest)
14 You'll feel better after a . . . . . (fortnight/holiday)
15 After a few . . . . the plane took off. (hours/delay)

6 ⊠
Countable and uncountable nouns

- Countable nouns are things that can be counted:
  a book, *two* cars, *three* planes

- Uncountable nouns cannot be counted as **one**, **two**, **three**, etc:
  milk, *water*, *flour* (⇨ exercise 15: if we want to count these things, we
  use **a litre of**, **a kilo of**, etc.)

* Note that *bread*, *cheese*, *butter*, *information*, *news*, *food*, and *money*
  are all uncountable nouns.

⇨ exercise 14 for **some** and **any**.

Copy these lists into your notebook and write '*C*' for countable, '*U*' for
uncountable:

apple	*C*	cheese		information	
water	*U*	tooth		butter	
boy		car		sugar	
milk		grass		tree	
table		person		garden	
pen		road		book	
bread		chair		news	
cup		bicycle		bus	
computer		hand		wine	
money		flour		house	

7   ⋆
Singular and plural

- To make a singular noun plural, add **s**:
  brother → *brother**s***; *car* → *car**s***; *house* → *house**s***

NOTES

* If the word ends in **ch**, **sh**, **x**, **o**, or **s**, add **es**:
  match → *match**es***; *box* → *box**es***

* If the word ends in **y**, change to **ies**:
  *bab**y*** → *bab**ies***; *lad**y*** → *lad**ies***

* Remember the common irregular plurals:
  men**, **women**, **children**, **people**, **teeth**, **feet

Copy this list into your notebook, and write the plurals:

brother	*brothers*	lady		woman	
sister		gentleman		box	
match		tooth		baby	
key		restaurant		person	
camera		house		man	
church		child		foot	
teacher		secretary		boy	
garden		student		table	
sandwich		bus		window	
door		cinema		banana	

8   ⋆⋆
Singular and plural

- To make singular words plural, add **s** (⇨ exercise 7).
  a) if the word ends in **o** or **s**, add **es**:
     tomato → *tomato**es***; *glass* → *glass**es***
     Note the exceptions *piano* → *pianos*; *stereo* → *stereos*;
     disco → *discos*; *video* → *videos*.

- b) if the the word is *half, leaf, thief, self, shelf, wife, wolf,* or *knife,*
     change the **f** or **fe** to **ve**:
     half → *hal**ves***; *wolf* → *wol**ves***

Note that most other words ending in **f** just add **s**:
roof → *roof***s**

● c) some animals have the same form in singular and plural:
deer → *deer*; *sheep* → *sheep*; *fish* → *fish* (or *fishes*)

＊ Note that the plural of ***mouse*** is ***mice***.

Write the plurals of the words given in brackets to complete these sentences:

1 Would you bring the bottle and some . . . ., please? (glass)
Would you bring the bottle and some glasses, please?
2 We cut the cake into . . . . . (half)
3 We bought some . . . . to eat with our . . . . . (tomato/sandwich)
4 They caught several . . . . that afternoon. (fish)
5 It was a shop selling . . . . and . . . . . (stereo/video)
6 Would you like some of these . . . .? (potato)
7 We saw a cartoon about . . . . and . . . . . (cat/mouse)
8 All the . . . . had different coloured . . . . . (house/roof)
9 It was autumn, and the . . . . were falling. (leaf)
10 Did you make these . . . .? (handkerchief)
11 We use several . . . . for painting the . . . . . (process/car)
12 They have some . . . . and a few . . . . . (chicken/sheep)
13 They visited several . . . . that night. (disco)
14 I've read her . . . ., but I haven't seen any of her . . . . . (book/play)
15 I bought some . . . . for the . . . . . (shelf/glass)
16 The . . . . came from several different . . . . . (boy/country)
17 I have heard strange . . . . about this place. (story)
18 They have a lot of . . . . at the moment. (worry)
19 Would you bring the . . . . and . . . .? (knife/fork)
20 The . . . . chased the . . . . for several miles. (wolf/deer)

9 ⊠
The indefinite article **a**

● **a** (or **an**) is used with countable nouns (⇨ exercise 6) to indicate one:
Can I have a cup of tea?
I've got a daughter and two sons.

● **a** is not used before a plural noun (NOT *I've got a sons*).

● **a** is not used before uncountable nouns (NOT *I want a petrol, please*).

Write **a**, **an**, or nothing to complete these sentences:

1 I'd like . . . . sandwich, please.
I'd like a sandwich, please.
2 He asked me for . . . . money.
He asked me for money.
3 They wanted . . . . information about the trains.
4 I'd like . . . . apple and . . . . orange, please.

5   They've got . . . . very big house.
6   Do you like . . . . fast cars?
7   We watched . . . . films all afternoon.
8   Have you got . . . . umbrella?
9   I asked for . . . . bread and . . . . cheese.
10   Are you drinking . . . . milk?
11   I had . . . . glass of water.
12   He gave me . . . . orange.
13   Is there . . . . telephone here?
14   We had . . . . eggs for breakfast.
15   I like . . . . coffee and . . . . tea.

10 ⋆
The indefinite article **a** and the definite article **the**

● **a** is used with countable nouns to indicate **one** (⟹ exercise 9):
  *I've got two bikes and **a** car.*
  *She's **a** lawyer.*
  *He's **a** teacher.*

● **the** is used:
  a) when a word is used a second time:
     *He gave me a knife and a spoon. **The** spoon was dirty.*
     *I bought a pen and some paper, but I left **the** pen in the shop.*
  b) when only one object exists:
     the earth
     the sun
     the River Thames

● **a** or **the** is not used before countries and towns:
  I live in Paris.
  He went to Italy.
  (NOT He went to the Italy)

*   But note: **the** USA, **the** USSR, **the** FRG, **the** Netherlands, **the** United
     Arab Emirates

Write **a**, **the**, or no article to complete these sentences:

1   She's . . . . journalist.
     She's a journalist.
2   We live in . . . . London.
     We live in London.
3   . . . . moon moves slowly round . . . . earth.
     The moon moves slowly round the earth.
4   We went to . . . . Venice and then to . . . . Rome.
5   . . . . sun is shining.
6   I'd like . . . . cup of coffee, please.
7   Have you got . . . . double room?
8   We went to . . . . Paris and saw . . . . Palace of Versailles.
9   He gave me a lighter and some cigarettes. . . . . lighter didn't work.

10 There was . . . . doctor and . . . . nurse in the room. . . . . nurse was sleeping.
11 She took . . . . sandwich and . . . . piece of cake, but didn't eat . . . . cake.
12 Yes, I work at this school. I'm . . . . teacher.
13 A man and two women were sitting in the car. I think . . . . man was Italian.
14 Did you see . . . . Pope when he came to England?
15 He offered me . . . . cigarette, but I refused.
16 Did you send me . . . . postcard when you were in . . . . Greece?
17 They had six cats and . . . . dog. I really liked . . . . dog.
18 Have you got . . . . match, please?
19 Have you been to . . . . USA?
20 She sent me . . . . letter and . . . . card. . . . . letter didn't arrive.
21 He's . . . . teacher. He's from . . . . Netherlands.
22 I had . . . . cup of tea and . . . . ice cream. . . . . tea was terrible.
23 Have you met Sally? She's . . . . . friend of mine.

11 ★★
The articles **a** and **the**

- **a** is used:
  a) to indicate **one** (⇨ exercises 9 and 10)
  b) to indicate cost, speed, or frequency:
      *twenty pence **a** kilo*
      *four times **a** day*
      *two hundred kilometres **an** hour*
  c) for certain numbers:
      ***a** hundred*; ***a** thousand*; ***a** couple*; ***a** dozen*

- **the** is used:
  a) when a word is used a second time (⇨ exercise 9)
  b) when talking about a known object:
      *I've just washed **the** car.* (= our car, or this car)
      *Where's **the** dog?* (= our dog, or the dog that is usually here)
      *We've made **the** beds.* (= our beds, or the beds here)
  c) in a general sense, with musical instruments:
      *Can you play **the** guitar?*
      *I like listening to **the** piano.*
  * But note: *I've just bought **a** guitar and **a** piano.*

- Usually, no article is used:
  a) with abstract nouns (*life, beauty, love*, etc), languages, and academic subjects (*history, Latin*, etc):
      Life isn't always easy.
      Latin is a difficult language to learn.
  b) with materials (*wine, coal, sugar*, etc) when they are considered in a general sense:
      Glass is a difficult material to cut.
      Gold is very expensive at the moment.

Note the difference between:
They were looking for gold. (= any gold)
*They found **the** gold.* (= the gold they were looking for)

c) before *school*, *home*, *work*, *church*, *bed*, and *hospital* in certain expressions:
We went to church.
She's at home.

Write **a**, **the**, or no article to complete these sentences:

1   She's a good musician: she plays . . . . piano beautifully.
    She's a good musician: she plays the piano beautifully.
2   I don't see him often, only once or twice . . . . month.
    I don't see him often, only once or twice a month.
3   Mary's not at . . . .office. I think she's gone . . . . home.
    Mary's not at the office. I think she's gone home.
4   Do you want to see Sarah? She's in . . . . garden.
5   I'm studying . . . . French and . . . . Italian.
6   I like Jayne, she has a lot of . . . . warmth.
7   It's time for the children to go to . . . . bed.
8   Where's . . . . dog? I want to go out for . . . . walk.
9   I don't use . . . . sugar when I'm cooking.
10 The machine is made of . . . . copper and . . . . steel.
11 Would you mind waiting for . . . . couple of minutes?
12 I think . . . . piano is one of the easiest instruments to play.
13 It's . . . . fast car. Its top speed is 150 miles . . . . hour.
14 I saw her when she was going to . . . . work.
15 There's someone at . . . . front door.
16 Do you like . . . . wine? I don't drink . . . . alcohol.
17 I'll have . . . . dozen eggs and . . . . loaf, please.
18 Coal is sixty dollars . . . . ton at the moment.
19 Have you done . . . . washing-up?
20 I think it's made of . . . . glass.
21 I like . . . . tea with . . . . milk in it.
22 I stayed at home last night and listened to . . . . radio.
23 Would you like . . . . cup of coffee?
24 They gave me . . . . diamond necklace.
25 When he was nineteen, he joined . . . . army.

12   ★★★
Words using **a**, **the**, or no article

●   Some words are used with **a**, **the**, or no article, depending on the meaning of the word, and whether it is thought of as definite (**the**), indefinite (**a**), or uncountable (⇨ exercises 9–11):

*I put **the** glass on the table.* (definite – a particular glass)
*I picked up **a** glass.* (indefinite – one of a number of glasses)
It's made of glass. (uncountable – glass as material)

Write **a**, **the**, or no article to complete these sentences:

tin
1   Could I have ten eggs and . . . . tin of peas?
     Could I have ten eggs and a tin of peas?
2   Put some money in . . . . tin by the door when you leave, please.
     Put some money in the tin by the door when you leave, please.
3   The cigarette lighter's made of . . . . tin.
     The cigarette lighter's made of tin.

wood
4   We knew that . . . . wood was a very expensive material at the time.
5   There's . . . . wood at the end of the road.
6   There are some rabbits living at the edge of . . . . wood.

paper
7   The boy who delivers . . . . paper is late today.
8   It was very strange, a shirt made of . . . . paper.
9   I generally read . . . . paper of some sort on the train.

chocolate
10   I won't take . . . . chocolate, thanks, although they look very nice.
11   Most doctors say . . . . chocolate is bad for you.
12   . . . . chocolates which I ate last night tasted very strange.

dress
13   She has a good sense of . . . . dress.
14   . . . . dress I liked was a bit too big for me.
15   I saw . . . . beautiful dress here yesterday.

experience
16   I'm afraid I didn't enjoy . . . . experience at all.
17   For this job you need . . . . experience with computers.
18   My first trip abroad was . . . . wonderful experience.

noise
19   I couldn't hear her because of . . . . noise of the train.
20   She heard . . . . strange noise behind the curtain.
21   What kind of . . . . noise are you talking about?

conversation
22   It was . . . . very embarrassing conversation.
23   I was trying to listen to . . . . conversation at the table next to me.
24   I always find . . . . conversation difficult in a foreign language.

13 ★★★
a, **the**, or no article: check

Choose the correct answer. '–' means no article is needed.

I could tell by *a/the/–* town hall clock that I was late, so I decided to catch *a/–* bus. It was *a/the/–* beautiful day; *a/the/–* sun was shining and there was *the/–* very little wind. I turned *the/–* corner, and walked down *a/the/–* main street.

    A/the/– couple of minutes later, I heard *a/the/–* noise, and *a/the/–* man wearing *a/the/–* grey leather jacket ran past me. At first, I thought he was trying to catch *the/–* bus which was waiting at *the/–* bus stop, but then *a/ the/–* policeman appeared, running at *a/–* some speed. He was obviously chasing *a/the/–* man in *a/the/–* leather jacket, and he was joined by another policeman, who was talking rapidly into *a/the/–* hand-held radio.

All three disappeared into *a/–* crowd of people, my bus arrived, and I got on. As *a/the/–* bus drove down *the/–* road, I saw *a/the/–* man again, walking casually through *a/the/–* crowd with his *the/–* coat over his shoulder. I could also see *a/the/–* second policeman, still talking into his radio. He was describing *a/–* man who no longer existed, *a/–* man wearing a jacket and running furiously: while *a/the/–* real criminal (if he was *a/–* criminal) walked slowly and casually into the station.

14 ☒
a, some, any

⇨ exercise 6 for the difference between countable and uncountable nouns.

● **a** is used with singular countable nouns:
   I'm waiting for a bus.

● **some** is used in *positive* sentences
   a) with plural countable nouns:
      ***Some** people arrived.*
      *I'd like a loaf and **some** eggs, please.*
   b) with uncountable nouns:
      *I bought **some** milk.*
      *I'd like **some** water, please.*

● **any** is used like **some**, but in *negative* sentences and *questions*
   a) with plural countable nouns:
      *Did **any** people arrive?*
      *I didn't buy **any** eggs.*
   b) with uncountable nouns:
      *Did you buy **any** milk?*
      *I didn't have **any** water.*

● **some** is used in offers:
   *Would you like **some** coffee?*
   *Would you like **some** tea?*

I've got (Would you like . . .?)	an apple some oranges some sugar
Have you got . . .? I haven't got	an apple any oranges any sugar

Write **a**, **some**, or **any** to complete these sentences:

1 I've got .... bananas and .... apple.
 I've got some bananas and an apple.
2 Did you bring .... bread?
 Did you bring any bread?
3 I'd like .... water, please.
4 Sorry, I haven't got .... matches.
5 I asked the waiter for .... tea.
6 I have .... information for you.
7 Didn't you bring .... money?
8 I sent her .... card from France.
9 Would you like .... coffee?
10 I want .... bread and .... kilo of cheese, please.
11 I have .... bad news for you.
12 At twelve o'clock we had .... food.
13 I bought .... books, but I didn't buy .... pen.
14 There aren't .... students here at the moment.
15 She didn't give me .... money.

15 ★★
Counting the uncountables

● It is not possible to say ~~one water, two flours,~~ etc.
 Uncountable objects are counted in two ways:
 a) in litres, kilos, etc:
  Could I have a kilo of potatoes?
  I need three litres of milk.
 b) by counting the containers that hold the uncountable noun:
  I'd like three bottles of lemonade, please.
  or by dividing the object into pieces, which are then counted:
  Would you like a piece of cake?

Write the correct word for each object:

1 a .... of lemonade
2 a .... of cake
3 a .... of bread
4 a .... of chocolates
5 a .... of peas
6 a .... of chocolate
7 a .... of Coca-Cola
8 a .... of jam
9 a .... of cigarettes
10 a .... of bread
11 a .... of milk
12 a .... of toothpaste

16 ★★
a few, a little and much, many, a lot of

● **a few** and **many** are used with plural countable nouns:
  *I've got **a few** friends.*
  *They haven't got **many** friends.*

● **a little** and **much** are used with uncountable nouns:
  *Could I have **a little** water, please?*
  *We haven't got **much** time.*

FORM

a) Plural countable

Positive

a few some a lot of	I've got a few friends. I've got some friends. I've got a lot of friends.

Negative and Question

any many a lot of	I haven't got any friends. I haven't got many friends. I haven't got a lot of friends. Have you got any/many/a lot of friends?

*   Note that it is sometimes possible to use **many** in the positive:
    *I've talked to them **many** times.*

b) Uncountables

Positive

a little some a lot of	I've got a little milk. I've got some milk. I've got a lot of milk.

Negative and Question

any much a lot of	I haven't got any milk. I haven't got much milk. I haven't got a lot of milk. Have you got any/much/a lot of milk?

Write **a few**, **a little**, **much** or **many** to complete these sentences. Do not use **some**, **any**, or **a lot of**:

1 There's some food, but not . . . . drink.
   There's some food, but not much drink.
2 . . . . people arrived before the party started, but not many.
   A few people arrived before the party started, but not many.
3 There's not . . . . food in the cupboard.
4 She hasn't got . . . . friends.
5 I'm sorry, I haven't got . . . . time.
6 The receptionist didn't give me . . . . information.
7 I can lend you . . . . money until tomorrow.
8 I asked him to put . . . . milk in my coffee.
9 I've seen her . . . . times this year, but not very often.
10 We only have . . . . petrol left.
11 She started feeling ill only . . . . days before the exam.
12 Not . . . . people come here in the winter.
13 Did they pay you . . . . money for working there?
14 There aren't . . . . towns in this part of England.
15 I didn't drink . . . . wine at the party.
16 There are only . . . . people at the beach.
17 I didn't have . . . . opportunity to talk to him.
18 The bank only lent me . . . . money.
19 Can I ask you . . . . questions?
20 The journey was a short one: it didn't take . . . . time.
21 Only . . . . students are going to fail the exam.
22 I don't think . . . . people will come tonight.
23 I haven't done . . . . work today.
24 I gave the cat . . . . milk.
25 I don't think I've made . . . . mistakes.

Adjectives and adverbs

17 ☒
Comparatives (**tall**, **taller**; **comfortable**, **more comfortable**)

● Adjectives with one syllable (*tall*, *great*, *short*, etc) add **er**:
   *tall → tall**er**; great → great**er**; short → short**er***
   Adjectives that end with **e** just add **r**:
   *wide → wide**r***
   a) if the word ends in one vowel + consonant, double the consonant:
   *thi**n** → thi**nner**; ho**t** → ho**tter**; bi**g** → bi**gger***
   b) if the word ends in two vowels and one consonant, do not double the consonant:
   *gr**ea**t → gr**ea**ter; p**oo**r → p**oo**rer*

c) if the word ends in **e**, just add **r**:
   large → *larger*
d) note the irregulars:
   good → **better**; **bad** → **worse**

17a Copy this list into your notebook and write the comparatives:

tall	*taller*	large		short	
thin		rich		hot	
wide		poor		cold	
long		young		warm	
good		big		cheap	
fat		bad		small	

● Adjectives with three syllables or more (*comfortable*, *beautiful*, *expensive*, etc) add **more**:
   comfortable → **more** *comfortable*; *beautiful* → **more** *beautiful*;
   expensive → **more** *expensive*

● When making comparisons, use **than**:
   *Mary's **taller than** John.*
   *John's **shorter than** Mary.*
   *The big television's **more expensive than** the small one.*
   *This chair's **more comfortable than** that one.*

17b Write the correct comparative for these sentences:

1   The Mississippi's . . . . the Thames. (long)
    The Mississippi's longer than the Thames.
2   This hotel's . . . . the other one. (comfortable)
    This hotel's more comfortable than the other one.
3   I think this shop is . . . . that one. (good)
4   The restaurant is . . . . the café. (expensive)
5   Simon's . . . . Mark. (old)
6   I think Scotland is . . . . England. (beautiful)
7   My brother's . . . . I am. (young)
8   I like this school because it's . . . . the other one. (big)
9   Accommodation here is . . . . in my country. (expensive)
10 The weather here is . . . . at home. (cold)
11 I think you're . . . . your father now. (tall)
12 His homework was . . . . mine. (bad)
13 This film is . . . . the one you wanted to see. (interesting)
14 The journey is . . . . I thought. (long)
15 This lesson is . . . . the last one. (difficult)

18 ★★
Comparatives

⇨ exercise 17 for adjectives with one syllable, and with three syllables or more.

● Adjectives with two syllables
a) generally use **more**:
careful → **more** *careful*; *stupid* → **more** *stupid*; *cautious* → **more** *cautious*
b) but if the adjective ends in **er**, **y**, or **ow**, add **er**:
clever → *cleverer*; *friendly* → *friendlier* (note: **y** changes to **i**); *pretty* → *prettier*; *narrow* → *narrower*

● The comparative of **little** is **less**, and of **few** is **fewer**:
I've got less money than she has.
There are fewer problems than there were before.

● Note the construction:
It's getting hotter and hotter.
It's getting more and more dangerous.

Write the comparative of the words given to complete the sentences. Add **than** where necessary:

1 He is . . . . he used to be. (helpful)
He is more helpful than he used to be.
2 It was slowly getting . . . . and . . . . . (hot)
It was slowly getting hotter and hotter.
3 I had . . . . time than I needed to finish the job. (little)
4 Peter gets . . . . and . . . . all the time. (selfish)
5 You seem . . . . you were yesterday. (happy)
6 My chair was getting . . . . and . . . . . (uncomfortable)
7 We need . . . . actors for this film. (young)
8 Do you think students are . . . . they used to be? (mature)
9 This road is . . . . and . . . . the other one. (long/dangerous)
10 Is the new car . . . . the old one? (expensive)
11 This system is . . . . the last one we had. (easy)
12 People here are . . . . they are at home. (polite)
13 The man was getting . . . . and . . . . . (angry)
14 The city is . . . . it used to be. (crowded)
15 She was feeling . . . . she had been earlier. (miserable)
16 Computers are . . . . nowadays. (complicated)
17 I think trains are . . . . and . . . . cars. (fast/comfortable)
18 We will have to think of a . . . . method. (good)
19 I'm beginning to feel . . . . about the results. (hopeful)
20 She seems to be getting . . . . and . . . . . (thin)

19 ★★
Comparatives: check

Complete these sentences, using the comparative form of the adjectives given:

1   It's . . . . here than in London. (hot)
    It's hotter here than in London.
2   She's . . . . than her brother. (imaginative)
    She's more imaginative than her brother.
3   He's . . . . than all the other students. (old)
4   This place is . . . . than the other one. (nice)
5   Do you think Pat is . . . . than Brian? (intelligent)
6   This school is . . . . than ours. (old-fashioned)
7   The computer was . . . . than I thought. (expensive)
8   The rooms are . . . . than they used to be. (clean)
9   He's . . . . than he was a year ago. (healthy)
10 Do you think English is . . . . than French? (difficult)
11 He eats a lot – he's getting . . . . and . . . . . (fat)
12 I think that girls are . . . . than boys. (mature)
13 Not many people are . . . . than he is. (dishonest)
14 His face was getting . . . . and . . . . . (red)
15 He was . . . . than I had ever seen him before. (angry)
16 Big cars are . . . . than small ones. (comfortable)
17 I think the book is . . . . than the film. (interesting)
18 Could I have a . . . . room, please? (big)
19 My exam was . . . . than I had thought. (bad)
20 The road becomes . . . . after three or four miles. (narrow)

20 ★★
Superlatives

●   Adjectives with one syllable add **est**:
    great → greatest; small → smallest; old → oldest

⇨   exercise 17 for spelling changes.

●   Adjectives with two syllables use **most**:
    *careful → **most** careful; patient → **most** patient*
    But two-syllable adjectives ending in **er**, **y** or **ow**, add **est**:
    *clever → cleverest; happy → happiest; (**y** changes to **i**); pretty → prettiest; narrow → narrowest*

●   Adjectives with three syllables or more use **most**:
    *expensive → **most** expensive; dangerous → **most** dangerous; comfortable → **most** comfortable*

USE

Superlatives are used to compare one person or thing with several others.

They are used with **the . . . in**, or **the . . . of**; sometimes they are used with just **the . . .**:

*This is **the** longest river **in** the world.*
*This is **the** most expensive car **of** them all.*
*This is **the** most expensive car here.*

Write the superlatives of the words given, using **in** or **of** where necessary:

1   This is . . . . the world. (big building)
    This is the biggest building in the world.
2   This is . . . . here. (comfortable chair)
3   He bought . . . . the shop. (expensive flowers)
4   I think she's . . . . the group. (good singer)
5   He's . . . . the company. (careful driver)
6   Who's . . . . the class? (old student)
7   It's . . . . I've ever seen. (bad film)
8   She's . . . . all the students. (intelligent)
9   It was . . . . I have ever heard. (beautiful music)
10 He's . . . . all the assistants. (helpful)
11 He's . . . . his class. (young)
12 This is . . . . the world. (poor country)
13 She's . . . . I've ever met. (strange person)
14 I didn't answer . . . . questions. (difficult)
15 Peter's . . . . them all. (old)

21 ★★
The qualification of comparatives and superlatives

This chair is	a bit a little a little bit much quite a lot a lot	cheaper more comfortable	than that one.

This chair is	as nearly as n't as n't nearly as twice/three times as	cheap comfortable	as that one.

It's	by far easily	the most expensive car in the world. the most expensive of all the cars I've seen.

Complete these sentences:

1   The weather is much . . . . it usually is at this time. (pleasant)
    The weather is much more pleasant than it usually is at this time.
2   Going by car took twice . . . . going by train. (long)
    Going by car took twice as long as going by train.

3   It was . . . . time of my life. (bad)
    It was the worst time of my life.
4   The train's a lot . . . . all the other ways of getting there. (fast)
5   This exam was a bit . . . . all the other tests. (easy)
6   I think English spelling is by far . . . . . (difficult)
7   The food isn't nearly . . . . it has been in the past. (good)
8   She's a bit . . . . her brother. (sensitive)
9   Flying's a lot . . . . going by car. (quick)
10 First class is much . . . . second. (expensive)
11 This is easily . . . . restaurant in London. (good)
12 Ellen was a bit . . . . she usually is. (cheerful)
13 He's not nearly . . . . his sister. (intelligent)
14 The journey was three times. . . .we had expected. (long)
15 The film wasn't . . . . I had thought it would be. (good)

22 ★★
Participial adjectives (**bored/boring**)

CONTRAST

● Note the difference:
  I was bored.
  The lesson was boring.
  It is not possible to say ~~The lesson was bored~~. It is possible to say:
  She was boring. (= so everybody was bored.)

Write these sentences, choosing the correct words:

1   It was a very (interesting/interested) performance.
    It was a very interesting performance.
2   We were all very (interesting/interested) in what he said.
    We were all very interested in what he said.
3   It was a very (tired/tiring) journey.
4   We were all very (worrying/worried).
5   The children are (frightening/frightened) by the animals.

6 Why do you look so (bored/boring) at school?
7 It was a terribly (excited/exciting) day.
8 Don't look so (worrying/worried).
9 We had a (tiring/tired) trip home.
10 It was an extremely (amused/amusing) programme.
11 What an (exciting/excited) idea!
12 It was the most (boring/bored) afternoon I can remember.
13 We were all feeling (tired/tiring).
14 Didn't you think it was an (amused/amusing) play?
15 The last half hour was a (worrying/worried) time.
16 I've never been so (frightened/frightening) in my life.

23 ⭐
Adverbs of manner

● Adverbs of manner (⇨ exercise 132) are formed from adjectives by adding **ly**:

quick → quickly; polite → politely; careful → carefully

● Note these irregulars: **good → well; hard → hard; fast → fast**.

He's a good worker. He works well.

She's a hard worker. She works hard.

She's a fast runner. She runs fast.

Copy this list into your notebook and write the *adverbs*:

quick	*quickly*	dangerous		bad	
slow		good		intelligent	
fast		hard		polite	
careful		clever		rude	
stupid		nice		brave	

24 ⭐⭐
Comparison of adverbs

● Most adverbs are used with **more** and **most**:
slowly → more slowly, most slowly
dangerously → more dangerously, most dangerously

* One-syllable adverbs add **er** and **est**:
hard → harder, hardest; fast → faster, fastest; loud → louder, loudest

*   The irregular comparisons are:

well	better	best		far	farther/	farthest/
badly	worse	worst			further	furthest
little	less	least				

Write the correct form of adverbs for these sentences:

1   She works . . . . than all the others. (hard)
    She works harder than all the others.
2   Of all the machines, this one works the . . . . . (good)
3   Couldn't you drive a bit . . . .? (careful)
4   I can't understand: would you ask him to speak . . . .? (clear)
5   They all behaved badly, but Pat behaved the . . . . . (bad)
6   John was shouting . . . . than everybody else. (loud)
7   I think I understand . . . . than the others. (good)
8   Susan climbed . . . . than the rest of us. (fast)
9   She gets up . . . . than everybody else in the house. (early)
10 Do you think they have acted . . . .? (stupid)

25 ★★
Adjectives and adverbs: check

Complete these sentences:

1   It was . . . . driving I have ever seen. (good)
    It was the best driving I have ever seen.
2   Peter sang . . . . than all the others. (loud)
    Peter sang louder than all the others.
3   The holiday wasn't . . . . as the one we had last year. (expensive)
    The holiday wasn't as expensive as the one we had last year.
4   She's a good student: she works . . . . than the others. (careful)
5   Would you play . . . ., please? I'm trying to sleep. (quiet)
6   Of all the people in the factory, Joan works . . . . . (efficient)
7   The weather isn't . . . . as I had expected. (bad)
8   This is the . . . . company in the world. (big)
9   She plays the piano . . . . than anyone else in her class. (beautiful)
10 Mr Jones is . . . . person in the village. (old)
11 Mark hit the ball very . . . . . (hard)
12 She runs . . . . than anyone else in the team. (fast)
13 Do you think older people drive . . . . than young people? (slow)
14 They all dance well, but John dances . . . . . (good)
15 This computer is nearly twice . . . . as the old one. (expensive)
16 He doesn't ski . . . . as his sister. (good)
17 This typewriter is . . . . than mine. (modern)
18 I think they both behaved very . . . . . (rude)
19 People aren't . . . . as they used to be. (thoughtful)
20 The government has acted . . . . than people had expected. (generous)

21 He spoke . . . ., but too . . . . . (clear/quick)
22 I waited . . . . than anyone else. (long)
23 I was . . . . player in our team. (old)
24 They all spoke French . . . ., but Patrick was . . . . of them all. (bad/bad)
25 I bought . . . . suit I could find. (cheap)
26 I chose the food for the party . . . . than I normally do. (careful)
27 Pat's . . . . driver in the company. (fast)
28 I walked . . . . out of the station. (quick)
29 Peter left . . . . than all the other people. (late)
30 This is . . . . chair I could find. (comfortable)

Verbs

The present tense

26 ★
Present Simple

FORM

Positive		Question			Negative		
I You We They	work.	Do	I you we they	work?	I You We They	do not (don't)	work.
He She It	works.	Does	he she it		He She It	does not (doesn't)	

* There is only one form of **you** in English, which is the same in singular and plural.

* Note the endings with **he**, **she**, and **it**. If the verb ends in **ss**, **sh**, **ch**, or **x**, add **es**:
  He finishes (*finish* ends in **sh**)
  She watches (*watch* ends in **ch**)

USE

● For something which is permanently true:
  I come from France.
  He doesn't speak Spanish.
  We live in London.

● For repeated actions or habits:
  I get up at six o'clock every day.
  What time do you leave work?
  I don't see them very often.

Rewrite each sentence as a *positive*, *negative*, or *question*, according to the instructions:

1 I visit my parents very often. (negative)
  I don't visit my parents very often.

2 Does he go to school every day? (positive)
He goes to school every day.
3 She comes from Germany. (question)
Does she come from Germany?
4 She goes to work by car. (question)
5 We watch television every night. (negative)
6 He doesn't walk to work every day. (positive)
7 She plays football every Saturday. (question)
8 He washes his car every week. (question)
9 They live in Australia. (question)
10 They go to school by bus. (question)
11 Does she finish work at five o'clock? (positive)
12 He goes to the cinema on Fridays. (question)
13 I come from Africa. (negative)
14 Does he live in this street? (positive)
15 He works in a restaurant. (question)
16 She gets up at five o'clock. (question)
17 They eat a lot. (negative)
18 Does he work here? (positive)

27 ⋆
Present Continuous

FORM

Positive

I am	→ I'm	
He She is It	→ He's She's It's	working.
We You are They	→ We're You're They're	

Question

Am I		
Is	he she it	working?
Are	we you they	

*Negative + **not***

I am	→ I'm	
He She is It	→ He's She's It's	not working.
We You are They	→ We're You're They're	

*Negative + **n't***

—	
He She isn't It	working.
We You aren't They	

USE

● For an action in progress now:
    I'm reading a grammar book now.
    What are you looking at?
    She isn't eating at the moment.

Rewrite each sentence as a *positive*, *negative*, or *question*, according to the instructions:

1 She's watching television now. (question)
    Is she watching television now?
2 He isn't staying at this hotel. (positive)
    He's staying at this hotel.
3 She's reading. (negative)
    She isn't reading.
4 They're working. (question)
5 He's writing a letter. (question)
6 He's eating. (negative)
7 I'm not working. (positive)
8 She's studying at the moment. (question)
9 I'm sleeping. (negative)
10 You're reading my newspaper. (question)
11 She's writing a letter. (question)
12 He's talking to Mary. (question)
13 They're not playing football. (positive)
14 He's listening to the radio. (question)
15 You're playing with my football. (question)
16 She's writing to her mother. (question)
17 We're listening to the stereo. (negative)
18 They aren't watching television. (positive)
19 He's reading. (negative)
20 They're eating. (question)

28 ⊠
Present Simple/Present Continuous

Write these sentences, putting the verbs into the correct tense:

1 She (read) at the moment.
    She's reading at the moment.
2 (You go) to work by car?
    Do you go to work by car?
3 I (not watch) television every night.
    I don't watch television every night.
4 I (not watch) television at the moment.
    I'm not watching television at the moment.
5 We (see) our parents every week.
6 (You listen) to the radio now?
7 I (not get up) at seven o'clock every morning.

8　Peter (talk) to Susan now.
9　(They work) in the restaurant?
10　She (listen) to the radio in her bedroom at the moment.
11　They (not come) to school every day.
12　(You work) now?
13　The children (go) to bed at eight o'clock.
14　I (leave) the office every day at five.
15　I'm sorry I can't talk to you now: I (go) out.
16　(Peter and Jane) work in London at the moment?
17　(Mary and Susan) drive to the office every day?
18　We (go) to the beach now.
19　(John listen) to the radio at the moment?
20　(Your parents sit) in the garden now?
21　The film (start) every night at eight o'clock.
22　They (not go) to the cinema very often.
23　(You go) into the office every month?
24　I (not study) at the moment.

29 ⊠
Present Continuous: short answers

'Are you working at the moment?' 'Yes, I am.'

FORM

Positive　　　　　　　　*Negative*

Yes,	I am.	No,	I'm not.
	he she it } is.		he she it } 's not. / he she it } isn't.
	we you they } are.		we you they } 're not. / we you they } aren't.

* Nouns → pronouns.
  *'Are **your parents** sleeping?'*
  *'Yes, **they** are.'*

* Positive short answers do not use contractions:
  Yes, I am. (NOT ~~Yes, I'm.~~)
  Yes, they are. (NOT ~~Yes, they're.~~)

* Contractions *are* used in negative short answers.
  Is she working?
  No, she isn't.

Someone is asking you questions. Copy these questions into your notebook and write the short answers. If two answers are possible, write the more likely one:

1	'Are you working at the moment?'	'*No. I'm not.*'
2	'Are your parents coming?'	'*Yes, they are.*'
3	'Are your sisters working now?'	'No, ...'
4	'Is John working at the moment?	'Yes, ...'
5	'Are they playing tennis?'	'No, ...'
6	'Are you reading this book?'	'Yes, ...'
7	'Is Mary going to school today?	'No, ...'
8	'Is Peter listening to the radio?'	'Yes, ...'
9	'Are they doing their homework now?'	'No, ...'
10	'Is the dog sleeping?'	'Yes, ...'

30 ⊠
Present Simple: short answers

FORM

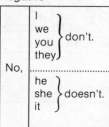

Positive   *Negative*

Yes,   I / we / you / they **do.**   he / she / it **does.**

No,   I / we / you / they **don't.**   he / she / it **doesn't.**

* Nouns → pronouns.
  '*Do **the men** want some tea?*'
  '*Yes, **they** do.*'

* Negative short answers can use the uncontracted form:
  *No, they **do not.*** (this is more emphatic)

Copy these questions into your notebook and write the short answers:

1	'Do you live here?'	'*Yes, I do.*'
2	'Does Mary work in this office?'	'*No, she doesn't.*'
3	'Does Stephen speak French?'	'No, ...'
4	'Do the teachers like your work?'	'Yes, ...'

5	'Do you understand the lessons?'	'No, ...'
6	'Do they visit you often?'	'No, ...'
7	'Do you like France?'	'Yes, ...'
8	'Do your parents live in London?'	'Yes, ...'
9	'Does your father like modern music?'	'No, ...'
10	'Does Judy drive to work?'	'Yes, ...'

31 ⋆
Present Simple and Continuous short forms: check

Someone is asking you questions. Copy these questions into your
notebook and write the short answers. If two answers are possible, write the
more likely one:

1	'Are your brothers working today?'	'*Yes, they are.*'
2	'Do you speak Italian?'	'*No, I don't.*'
3	'Do you like this school?'	'Yes, ...'
4	'Do you go to school in London?'	'Yes, ...'
5	'Is your mother watching television?'	'Yes, ...'
6	'Do you go to school on Sundays?'	'No, ...'
7	'Are your parents staying here?'	'No, ...'
8	'Does the dog sleep in your bedroom?'	'No, ...'
9	'Do you get up at eight o'clock?'	'Yes, ...'
10	'Is Mary listening to the stereo?'	'Yes, ...'
11	'Does the film start at six o'clock?'	'No, ...'
12	'Are the children playing football?'	'Yes, ...'
13	'Does Susan drive to work?'	'Yes, ...'
14	'Are you reading?'	'No, ...'
15	'Am I reading your paper?'	'Yes, ...'
16	'Are they doing the washing-up?'	'Yes, ...'
17	'Do you come to work by bike?'	'No, ...'
18	'Is John watching television?'	'No, ...'

32 ⋆⋆
Verbs using Present Simple rather than Present Continuous

USE
● Certain verbs generally use only the *simple* form, and are not used with
the *continuous*. These are verbs which do not describe activities. They
include:

  a) verbs of thinking and understanding:
   I believe you.
   I don't understand.
   What do you think?

  b) verbs of seeing, hearing, feeling, etc:
   I don't like him.
   How do you feel?
   I want to go.

*   These verbs can use the *present continuous* when they become
     activity verbs:
     *Be quiet, please: I'm **thinking**.* (Here, **thinking** is an activity, like
     working.)
     *I'm **seeing** the President tomorrow.* (**seeing** = **meeting**)

*   There is a difference between these verbs:
     listen – hear; **look – see**; **watch – see**
     Listen, **watch**, and **look** are deliberate activities, and can use the
     present continuous:
     I'm listening to the radio.
     Hear and **see** are not deliberate activities, and do not usually use the
     continuous.

⇨   exercise 66 for an explanation of *simple* and *continuous aspect*.

Write the correct form of the verb for these sentences:

1   You're very quiet. What (do you think / are you thinking) about?
     You're very quiet. What are you thinking about?
2   What (are you thinking / do you think) about the new sports centre?
     What do you think about the new sports centre?
3   I'm sorry (I'm not agree / I don't agree) with you.
4   (Are you looking / Do you look) for me?
5   (Do you prefer / Are you preferring) walking to cycling?
6   (I don't like / I'm not liking) him at the moment.
7   (I hear / I'm hearing) you're leaving us.
8   I'm afraid (I'm not remembering / I don't remember) where we met.
9   (Do you listen / Are you listening) to the radio at the moment?
10   (I'm hating / I hate) cold evenings.
11   (I'm not looking forward / I don't look forward) to my holiday.
12   (They're looking / They look) at clothes at the moment.
13   Why (aren't you agreeing / don't you agree) with the idea?
14   What (is this meaning? / does this mean?)
15   (I'm not understanding / I don't understand) the lessons.
16   (I never agree / I'm never agreeing) with what he says.
17   (He knows / He's knowing) you're wrong.
18   (They watch / They're watching) us.

33 ★★
Present Simple and Present Continuous:
permanent and temporary

CONTRAST

●   The *present simple* is used to express permanent facts ⇨ exercise 26.

●   The *present continuous* is sometimes used as a contrast to *present
     simple*, to show temporary events:
     *I **live** in Mexico, though **I'm staying** in Texas at the moment.*
     *I'm living in Paris just now, but **I come** from Belgium.*

Write these sentences, putting the verbs into the correct tense:

1 I (live) in Washington, though I (stay) in London at the moment.
   I live in Washington, though I'm staying in London at the moment.
2 The car isn't here today because Sheila (use) it. She generally (use) the bus, but the drivers are on strike.
3 We usually (stay) at home on Fridays, but we came out tonight because the children (have) a party.
4 I (come) from Scotland, though I (live) in London just now.
5 I (stay) with my parents at the moment, though I (have) my own flat.
6 They usually (work) at the weekends, though they (not work) at the moment.
7 He (teach) in a language school, though he (work) in a factory at the moment because the school's on holiday.
8 The business usually (make) money, though it (do) rather badly just now.
9 I usually (work) at night, though I (have) a holiday at the moment.
10 I (not speak) French, though I (study) it at the moment.

NOTES

⇨ exercise 59 for **when**, **as soon as**, **before**, **until** + *present simple*.
⇨ exercises 79 and 83 for **if** + *present simple*.
⇨ exercise 53 for *present continuous* used as *future*.
⇨ exercise 133 for *present simple* + **usually**, **often**, **sometimes**, etc.

The past tense

34 ☒
Past Simple: question and negative

FORM

● The *past simple* question forms are the same for all persons (**I**, **you**, **he**, **she**, etc) and all verbs:

Did	Subject	Infinitive
Did	I he she it we you they	leave? go? stay?

● The *past simple* negative forms are the same for all persons and all verbs:

Subject	**did not**	Infinitive
I He She It We You They	did not didn't	leave. go. stay.

USE

⇨ exercise 35.

Write these sentences in the *past simple*, keeping them as questions or negatives:

1 Do they agree?
   Did they agree?
2 They don't drive.
   They didn't drive.
3 When do they go?
4 Where do they work?
5 Do you understand?
6 I don't know.
7 He doesn't like it.
8 What do you think?
9 She doesn't live here.
10 How much does it cost?
11 When do you get up?
12 I don't swim.
13 She doesn't speak Spanish.
14 We don't understand.
15 When do they leave?
16 When does he go to school?
17 Do you like Germany?
18 When do you go out?
19 She doesn't smoke.
20 He doesn't know.

35 ⭐
Past Simple: positive – regular verbs

FORM

● Regular verbs have the same form for all persons (**I**, **you**, **he**, **she**, etc):

Subject	Infinitive + **ed**
I He She It We You They	stayed.

● Irregular verbs are different in the positive ⇨ exercise 36.

- Remember to use the infinitive without **ed** for questions and negatives
  ⇨ exercise 34.
  Did you stay? (NOT *Did you stayed?*)

- Spelling:
  a) verbs ending in **e** add only **d**:
     I love → *I loved*
  b) verbs ending in **y** change **y** to **ied**:
     I try → *I tried*
  c) most verbs ending in a single vowel + single consonant change to
     single vowel + double consonant:
     I travel → *I travelled*
     We stop → *We stopped*

USE

- For a past action or state. The action can be a short one:
  I asked a question.
  She missed the bus.

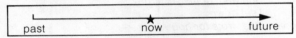

or a long one:
I walked for hours.
I lived here for years.

Change the verbs into the *past simple*, keeping them as positives,
negatives, or questions:

1	He lives here.	12	Do you drive to school?
	He lived here.	13	I don't like him.
2	Do you work here?	14	Do you miss your parents?
	Did you work here?	15	We love Spain.
3	I don't like the film.	16	John studies music.
4	She hates the hotel.	17	Where do you live?
5	We don't live there.	18	What does he study?
6	Does he play the piano?	19	Where does she work?
7	I love Paris.	20	We don't like London.
8	He doesn't work very hard.	21	They hate waiting.
9	She travels a lot.	22	They work in a factory.
10	He walks everywhere.	23	Do you live in this house?
11	I don't study English.	24	Does your husband work here?

36 ☒
Past Simple: positive – irregular verbs

FORM

● Irregular verbs have the same form for all persons (**I**, **you**, **he**, **she**, etc):

Subject	Past Simple
I He She It We You They	went.

● Irregular verbs are irregular in the *past simple* in the *positive* only (not in the negative or question form):
  go → went   *She went home yesterday.*
  sit → sat   *I sat down.*
  write → wrote   *She wrote for hours.*

USE

⇨ exercise 35.

Look at these irregular forms (⇨ exercise 68 for a longer list):

went (go)	gave (give)
sat (sit)	had (have)
came (come)	got up (get up)
wrote (write)	ate (eat)
ran (run)	drank (drink)

Using the verbs above complete these sentences:

1 I . . . . a few letters yesterday.
   I wrote a few letters yesterday.
2 He . . . . at six o'clock this morning.
3 They . . . . home late last night.
4 She . . . . a headache yesterday.
5 I was hungry so I . . . . some bread and cheese.
6 They came into my office and . . . . down.
7 We . . . . some water.
8 I was late so I . . . . to work.
9 She . . . . abroad last week.
10 They . . . . him some money.

37 ⊠
Past Simple: positive

37a Copy these irregular verbs into your notebook and write the *past simple positive:*

buy		forget		see	
catch		give		sit	
choose		go		speak	
come		know		take	
do		make		tell	
drink		put		think	
eat		read		understand	

37b Write these sentences, putting the verbs given into the *past simple*. Remember that the *infinitive* is used for questions and negatives:

1   I . . . . some new clothes last week. (buy)
    I bought some new clothes last week.
2   What time . . . . last night? (they come)
    What time did they come last night?
3   I . . . . his question. (not understand)
    I didn't understand his question.
4   I . . . . he was wrong. (think)
5   . . . . a lot at the party? (you eat)
6   I . . . . the bus this morning. (not catch)
7   I . . . . my keys yesterday. (forget)
8   . . . . you about the meeting? (they tell)
9   Peter . . . . the washing-up last night. (do)
10 They . . . . anything at the disco. (not drink)
11 I . . . . your suitcase in your bedroom. (put)
12 We . . . . it was your birthday. (not know)
13 . . . . to the office yesterday? (you go)
14 They . . . . her a present when she left. (give)
15 We . . . . their letters. (read)
16 He . . . . a bad mistake. (make)
17 They . . . . me about your problem. (tell)
18 . . . . the money from the office? (you take)
19 I . . . . anything strange. (not see)
20 She . . . . to me. (not speak)
21 We . . . . what he wanted. (understand)
22 They . . . . some food and drink. (buy)
23 She . . . . his telephone number. (know)

38 ⭐⭐
Past Continuous

FORM

Positive		*Question*		*Negative*		

I						
He	was					
She						
It		working.				
We	were					
You						
They						

	I			
Was	he			
	she			
	it	working?		
Were	we			
	you			
	they			

I	was not	
He	(wasn't)	
She		
It		working.
We	were not	
You	(weren't)	
They		

USE

● To describe a past action at some point between its beginning and its end. The *past continuous* is often interrupted by the *past simple*:

I **was having** a bath when the phone **rang**.

John **arrived** when I **was eating**.

I **was listening** to the radio when I **had** an idea.

* Note the difference between:
a) *When she arrived, we had dinner.*
b) *When she arrived, we were having dinner.*
The time order for (a) is *arriving* then *having dinner*.
The time order for (b) is *having dinner*, during which *she arrived*.

When she arrived, we were having dinner.

38a Look at these sentences and answer the questions by choosing A or B:

1   When I saw them, they were playing football.
     Which happened first?
     A I saw them   B they were playing football
     Answer: *B*

2   When she telephoned, I was having a bath.
    Which happened first?
    A the telephone call   B the bath
3   They were watching television when I visited them.
    Which happened first?
    A They were watching television   B I visited them
4   I was walking into the house when I heard the noise.
    Which happened first?
    A I was walking into the house   B I heard the noise
5   I walked into the house when I heard the noise.
    Which happened first?
    A I walked into the house   B I heard the noise
6   We left the party when the police arrived.
    Which happened first?
    A We left the party   B the police arrived
7   We were leaving the party when the police arrived.
    Which happened first?
    A We were leaving the party   B the police arrived
8   I made the beds when Joan and Ian got here.
    Which happened first?
    A I made the beds   B Joan and Ian got here
9   I was making the beds when Joan and Ian got here.
    Which happened first?
    A I was making the beds   B Joan and Ian got here
10 I was getting into my car when I heard the shot.
    Which happened first?
    A I was getting into my car   B I heard the shot

38b Complete these sentences by putting the verbs into the *past
continuous* or the *past simple*:

1   I . . . . television when the phone rang. (watch)
    I was watching television when the phone rang.
2   When the ambulance came we . . . . him into it. (carry)
3   She . . . . her car when she suddenly felt ill. (drive)
4   When he saw me he . . . . off the wall. (fall)
5   We . . . . to the radio when it suddenly stopped working. (listen)
6   Why . . . . cards when he walked into the office? (you play)
7   . . . . you when you gave them the money? (they thank)
8   . . . . when you turned on the gas? (you smoke)
9   When I arrived, they . . . . hello but continued working. (say)
10 When I got to the hospital, she . . . . in the waiting room. (sit)

39 ★★
Past Simple and Past Continuous: check

Write **did**, **was**, or **were** to complete these sentences:

1   I . . . . .n't like it.
    I didn't like it.

2   They .... enjoying themselves.
They were enjoying themselves.
3   .... you have a good time?
4   What time .... you leave?
5   .... he staying in a hotel?
6   I .... n't eating.
7   What .... you do then?
8   Why .... they sitting there?
9   What .... they doing?
10 What .... you say?
11 Why .... he working late last night?
12 They .... n't playing cards.
13 She .... n't understand.
14 I .... n't having a bath.
15 What .... the dog eating?
16 They .... n't buy anything.
17 .... you like the film?
18 Why .... n't you go to school?
19 .... you talking to somebody?
20 .... they write you a letter?

40 ★★
Past Simple and Past Continuous: short answers

'*Were you working last night?*' '*Yes, I was.*'
'*Did Mary ask you to work late?*' '*No, she didn't.*'

FORM

Past Simple

Subject + **did**	
I He She It We You They	did. didn't.

Past Continuous

Subject + **was/were**	
I He She It	was. wasn't.
We You They	were. weren't.

*   The short answer to *'Did you like it?'* is *'Yes I did.'* (NOT ~~Yes. I liked.~~)

Someone is asking you questions. Write the short answers:

1   'Were you sitting here yesterday?'   *'No, I wasn't.'*
2   'Did she see the accident?'   *'Yes, she did.'*
3   'Did you leave the hotel last night?'   'No, ...'
4   'Was he working when you arrived?'   'Yes, ...'
5   'Were they eating when you phoned?'   'Yes, ...'
6   'Did your father buy another car?'   'No, ...'
7   'Did you see that letter for you?'   'Yes, ...'
8   'Were your brothers sleeping when you left?'   'Yes, ...'
9   'You didn't see the accident, then.'   'No, ...'
10 'They weren't waiting for you.'   'No, ...'
11 'Did you like the present?'   'Yes, ...'
12 'Did the children have a good time?'   'Yes, ...'
13 'Was Susan driving when you saw her?'   'No, ...'
14 'Did he speak to you?'   'Yes, ...'
15 'Did you do the washing-up?'   'Yes, ...'
16 'Were you doing your homework when I phoned?' 'Yes, ...'
17 'Was your father washing the car?'   'Yes, ...'
18 'Did you understand what he was saying?'   'No, ...'
19 'Was she leaving when you got there?'   'Yes, ...'
20 'Did your sister lose her purse yesterday?'   'Yes, ...'

41 ★★★
Past Continuous as narrative

The *past continuous* is often used in a *past simple* narrative to describe the background history or environment:

> It was a typical summer afternoon: the sun was beating down, the cars were creeping slowly round the corner of the park. Five or six children were playing in the stream by the fountain, jumping in and out of the water, their laughter mixing with the noise of the traffic. All the world was wearing shorts, or T-shirts, or bathing-costumes: yet Walter Harrison, sitting on a park bench in his overcoat, was feeling cold and lonely. 'Where will it all end?' he thought, as he watched the children splashing and laughing. After a few minutes, he got up and walked through the park gates. His adventure was about to begin . . .

Write the verbs in this story in the *past simple* or *past continuous*. Sometimes both tenses are possible. Choose the one that is most likely:

> He stopped just before putting his key in the front door. Something was happening in the back garden . . . Quietly, he crept around the side of the house and (look) through the gate. Two men (stand) at the back of the house, holding a ladder. A third man was at the top of the ladder, and a fourth inside the house: he (pass) furniture through the window to his partner, who then (give) it to his friends below. All four (work)

quietly and efficiently, and the pile of furniture in the garden (get) bigger by the minute. Derek (can not) believe his eyes: the team of strangers (empty) his entire flat, and they (behave) as if this was the most normal thing in the world! He (cough) loudly, and then (say) 'Excuse me!' – and the man at the top of the ladder (drop) his portable TV onto the concrete below.

⇨   exercise 66 for an explanation of the *simple* and *continuous aspects*.

42 ★
Present Perfect

FORM

| **has/have** + *past participle* |

Positive

I We You They	have ('ve)	finished.
He She It	has ('s)	

Question

Have	I we you they	finished?
Has	he she it	

Negative

I We You They	have not (haven't)	finished.
He She It	has not (hasn't)	

USE

● The *present perfect* describes the indefinite past:
  I've been to Paris.
  I've seen this film before.
  They've met my parents.
  The past is indefinite because the time it happened is not important, or because we do not know when it happened. Note the difference between:
  I went to Paris last year. (definite time – *past simple*)
  I've been to Paris. (at some time in my life – indefinite time – *present perfect*).

- The *present perfect* is often used to describe personal experience:
  I've been to Berlin.
  She's met a lot of famous people.
  I've heard this music before.

- The question form is often **Have you ever . . .?** (= in your life?)
  Have you ever been to Paris?

- The *present perfect* is not used with past time words (**last night**, **yesterday**, **in 1984**, etc). It is not possible to say ~~I've seen him yesterday.~~

* Note the difference between:
  *She's **gone** to Sweden.* (= and she's there now)
  *She's **been** to Sweden.* (= but she isn't there now)

42a Write the correct form of the *present perfect* to complete these sentences:

1 .... to Rome? (you ever be)
  Have you ever been to Rome?
2 .... this film before. (I see)
  I've seen this film before.
3 .... in an office. (she never work)
4 .... in an aeroplane. (I never be)
5 .... to Germany? (he ever be)
6 .... my parents? (you met)
7 .... in the theatre? (you ever work)
8 .... to all the capital cities of Europe. (she be)
9 .... this book. (I read)
10 .... the new Superman film? (you see)
11 .... abroad. (we never be)
12 .... a British policeman before. (they never see)
13 .... in a foreign country? (they ever live)
14 .... the President. (they meet)
15 .... to Brazil. (I never be)

42b **'s** in a verb can be short for **is** or **has**:
  He's tired. / It's dead. / She's thirsty. (= is)
  He's gone. / It's disappeared. / She's left. (= has)

Are these contractions **is** or **has**?

1 He's tired. (= is)
2 She's arrived.
3 It's escaped.
4 She's ill.
5 He's eaten.
6 She's worried.
7 He's left the country.
8 She's stopped working.
9 He's had a cold.
10 It's died.

43 ⊠
Present Perfect/Past Simple: check

Write these sentences, putting the verbs into the *present perfect* or *past simple*:

1   I (read) that book.
    I've read that book.
2   She (go) home three days ago.
    She went home three days ago.
3   I (met) Mr and Mrs Shelley.
4   She (start) school in 1984.
5   I (leave) the office early last night.
6   He (see) the film.
7   (You be) to Austria?
8   (You see) the film on TV last night?
9   When (you arrive) in London?
10 John (be) to Germany before.
11 (You read) this book before?
12 I (not see) him yesterday.
13 I never (go) anywhere by plane.
14 (You hear) their new record? It's the best they've ever made.
15 I (not know) about the disco last night.

44 ⊠
Present Perfect + **for/since**

USE

- The *present perfect* + **for/since** is used when something started in the past and is continuing now:
  *I've worked here **for** six years.* (and I'm working here now)
  *He's lived here **since** 1980.* (and he's living here now)

* **for** = during a period of time:
   *I've lived here **for** six years.*
   *I've worked there **for** two months.*

	for six years	for three years	for two months	now
for:	├─	├─	├─	(April
since:	since 1979	since 1982	since February	1985)

* **since** = from a point in time:
   *I've lived here **since** 1979.*
   *I've worked there **since** February.*

* Note the difference between the *present perfect* and the *past simple*:
   *He's worked here **for** six months.* (= he's working here now)
   *He worked here **for** six months.* (= he's not working here now)

* It is not possible to say *~~He worked here since 1980.~~*

Write these sentences, choosing **for** or **since**:

1 I've worked here (for/since) six years.
 I've worked here for six years.
2 I lived here (for/since) three months.
3 I've worked in the factory (for/since) 1970.
4 He's been abroad (for/since) five years.
5 I studied French (for/since) twelve years.
6 I've known her (for/since) 1982.
7 I've lived here (for/since) I was a child.
8 We've been in Paris (for/since) we were married.
9 I've known them (for/since) years.
10 We practised (for/since) months.

Write these sentences choosing **for** or **since**, and putting the verb into the *past simple* or *present perfect* as necessary:

11 I (study) (for/since) six years, but then I stopped.
 I studied for six years, but then I stopped.
12 She (work) for me (for/since) she left school.
 She's worked for me since she left school.
13 I (work) in the restaurant (for/since) six months, but then it closed.
14 I (live) here (for/since) I was a little girl.
15 He (be) in prison now (for/since) three years.
16 I (not see) him (for/since) he left the office.
17 I (not see) her (for/since) several years, and then I met her again.
18 We (be) in Vienna (for/since) 1950.
19 I (work) here (for/since) seven years, but it's time to leave now.
20 I (live) in England (for/since) 1983.

45 ★★
Present Perfect

USE

The *present perfect* is used to show a connection in the speaker's mind between the past and the present. This occurs in two main ways:

a) *the unfinished past:*
– by referring to something that started in the past and is continuing now:
 I've lived here for seven years. (and I live here now)
 I've worked here since 1984. (and I work here now)

 ⇨ exercise 44.

– or describing something that happened, when the period of time that we are referring to has not finished:
 I've read two books this week.
 I've seen him twice today.
 She's telephoned three times this morning.

b) *the indefinite past:* referring to the past with no definite time (⇨ exercise 42). It is connected to the present in some way, and is often used in the following situations:

— describing something that happened in the past, when the result can be seen in the present:

He's painted his house.

Someone's taken my wallet.

She's bought a new car.

— describing something that happened recently, often when giving 'news':
Two men have escaped from a prison in London.
The Prime Minister has arrived in Australia.
— with certain words (**just, yet, already**):
He's just gone out.
I've told you already.
Have you done your homework yet?
— describing personal experience:
I've been to Paris.
He's never been abroad.
— describing personal experience with superlatives or ordinals:
She's the most intelligent person I've met.
This is the third time we've complained.

The sentences below belong to one or more of the categories above. Write them in your notebook, putting the verbs into the *present perfect*:

1   She . . . . ill for several months. (be)
       She's been ill for several months.
2   This is the nicest restaurant I . . . . . (see)
3   Three people . . . . the company this week. (leave)
4   I . . . . three letters already. (write)
5   We . . . . two holidays this year. (have)
6   There . . . . a revolution in San Serife. (be)
7   I . . . . that film. (see)
8   Someone . . . . your front gate! (knock down)
9   It's the first time I . . . . here. (be)
10   . . . . Indonesian food? (you ever eat)
11   . . . . your homework yet? (you do)
12   This is the fourth time he . . . . my car. (damage)
13   You . . . . a shave! (have)
14   She's got the best voice I . . . . . (ever hear)
15   He . . . . here since eight o'clock. (be)
16   The Prime Minister . . . . for a meeting with the President. (ask)
17   She . . . . . (just go out)
18   I . . . . . (never smoke)
19   This is the first time the children . . . . on a plane. (be)
20   . . . . Mary already? (you see)

46 ★★
Present Perfect with **just**, **yet**, and **already**

* Note the position of **just**, **yet**, and **already**:
  just goes before the *past participle*:
  He's just gone. / Has he just gone?
  yet goes after the *past participle*:
  Has she gone yet?
  already goes before or after the *past participle* (+ *object*):
  She's already left. / She's left already. / She's left the house already.
  Has she already left? / Has she left already? / Has she left the house already?
* **yet** is used only with *negatives* and *questions*:
  She hasn't phoned yet.
  Has she phoned yet?

Write these sentences putting the words in brackets in the correct place. If two answers are possible, write them both:

1 I'm sorry, she's gone – she went some time ago. (already)
   I'm sorry, she's already gone – she went some time ago.
   I'm sorry, she's gone already – she went some time ago.
2 Have you finished? It's time to go. (yet)
3 I haven't done my homework. (yet)
4 I've told her several times that I can't come. (already)
5 You've missed her – if you hurry, you'll catch her in the street. (just)
6 Have you finished painting the house? (yet)
7 I've said that I'm not going to be here tomorrow. (already)
8 I haven't explained. (yet)
9 Have you got your passport? (already)
10 He's told me that I've got the sack. (just)

47 ★★★
Past Simple and Present Perfect

Write the story, putting the verbs in brackets into the *present perfect* or *past simple*. If two answers are possible, write the more likely one:

Ann Jones is one of the most interesting people I (meet): she is only twenty-five, but she (travel) to over fifty different countries. Five years ago, she (be) a typist in Birmingham, but she (decide) to give up her job and see the world. Since then, her life (change) completely.

The first time she (go) abroad was seven years ago, when she (be) just eighteen. She (take) a boat to France and then (hitch-hike) around Europe for five weeks. She (visit) Europe many times since that first trip, of course, but this holiday (be) the one which (make) her start travelling. She (never forget) the excitement of those five weeks – although it was not all enjoyable. When she (be) in Munich, somebody (steal) her purse: she (lose) all her money, and (have) to work in a restaurant for a fortnight. She (make) some good friends there, however, and (return) several times since then.

How did she find the money for her travels? After her first trip abroad, she (go) home and (work) for two years, saving all the time. Now she travels continually, finding work when her money gets low. She (make) a lot of friends, she says, and (learn) quite a few languages. Although she (have) occasional difficulties and (often be) sick, she (never think) about giving up her travels. 'The first time I (go) abroad (change) my life,' she says, 'and I (want) to travel ever since.'

48 ★★
Present Perfect Continuous

FORM

> **has/have** + **been** + *verb* **-ing**

Positive		
I We You They	have ('ve)	been waiting.
He She It	has ('s)	

Question		
Have	I we you they	been waiting?
Has	he she it	

Negative		
I We You They	have not (haven't)	been waiting.
He She It	has not (hasn't)	

USE

● Frequently used with **how long**, **for** and **since** (⇨ exercise 44 for difference between **for** and **since**).
I've been studying English since I was a child.
How long have you been waiting?

● To describe activities which were happening until this moment or a very short time ago:
'You look tired.' 'Yes, I've been working all night.'
'Why are you so dirty?' 'I've been playing football.'

* Note that this tense is not used with **to be** or with verbs that do not normally take the *continuous* (⇨ exercise 32 for verbs not usually used in continuous).

Write the verbs in the *present perfect continuous*:

1   'What (you do) today?' 'I (play) tennis.'
    'What have you been doing today?' 'I've been playing tennis.'
2   'How long (you study) English?'
3   'Oh, David! I (look) for you!'
4   'Pat (live) here for twenty-five years.'
5   'I'm tired. We (walk) all day.'
6   'How long (you learn) to drive?'
7   'I (wait) here for ages.'
8   'She's irritable because she (work) too hard.'
9   'They (watch) the football since three o'clock.'

10 'Why (you see) your parents so much recently?'
11 'The children look tired. What (they do)?'
12 'She should pass the exam. She (study) for weeks.'
13 'Your mother sends her love. I (just speak) to her on the phone.'
14 'I (work) here since I was eighteen.'
15 'I'm tired. I (travel) for hours.'

49 ★★
Present Perfect Simple and Continuous

CONTRAST

● The *present perfect simple* is used when the action is complete and the final achievement is important:
I've run six kilometres.
(NOT ~~I've been running six kilometres~~.)

● The *present perfect continuous* is used when the activity is important. We are interested in how someone has been spending time, and the achievement is not important:
I've been running. (NOT ~~I've run.~~)

Write the dialogue putting the verbs into the *present perfect simple* or *continuous* as necessary:

JULIA: Gosh, it (be) busy this morning, hasn't it?
PAT: Yes, you look exhausted. What (you do)?
JULIA: I (not stop) all morning. I (write) letters, (answer) the phone, (do) the filing . . . . it (be) impossible.
PAT: It (be) the same for me. My phone (ring) all morning, I (write) five letters . . . and I (interview) three people for that secretarial job.
JULIA: Have you? Oh, I (interview) one as well. And I (send) off another ten application forms to people who want them. It seems to be very popular.
PAT: It does, doesn't it? I can't think why. Four people (phone) me about it this morning.
JULIA: Have they? . . . Oh, and I (look) through that letter, you know, the one the managing director sent to all the staff . . .
PAT: Oh, yes, I (already read) that. Not very interesting, is it?
JULIA: No . . . I think (read) it all before . . .

50 ★★
Past Perfect

FORM

> **had/'d** + *past participle*

Positive			Question			Negative		
I He She It We You They	'd had	gone.	Had	I he she it we you they	gone?	I He She It We You They	hadn't had not	gone.

USE

● To describe a time before the past time being discussed:
*I **had spoken** to Mr Johnson before the meeting began.*

● To describe a period of time leading up to the past time being discussed:
*By 1984, we **had waited** seven years for an answer.*

*   Note the difference between *past simple/past simple*:
*I **got** to the stadium at 7.15, and the game **started** at 7.30.* (= the game started *after* I arrived)
and *past simple/past perfect*:
*I **got** to the stadium at 7.45, but the game **had started** at 7.30.* (= the game started *before* I arrived)

Write the sentences putting one verb in each sentence into the *past simple*, and the other verb into the *past perfect*:

1   When the police (arrive) the car (go).
    When the police arrived the car had gone.
2   When I (get) to the shop it (close).
3   They (eat) everything by the time I (arrive) at the party.
4   When we (leave) the beach the rain (already start).
5   I (try) telephoning her several times but she (leave) the country.
6   When I (find) my purse someone (take) the money out of it.
7   The car (go) when I (look) into the street.
8   The patient (already die) by the time I (see) her.
9   All the garages (close) by the time we (cross) the border.
10 (You already leave) when the trouble (start)?
11 I (not finish) getting off the train when it suddenly (start) moving.

12 (You already complain) to the manager when the waiter (be) rude?
13 We (not finish) cleaning the machine, but we (decide) to stop work.
14 They (decide) to get married last month, although they (know) each other for only six weeks.

51 ★★★
Past Perfect Continuous

FORM

had/'d + been + verb -ing

Positive

I He She It We You They	had ('d)	been working.

Question

Had	I he she it we you they	been working?

Negative

I He She It We You They	had not (hadn't)	been working.

USE

● As *present perfect continuous*, but changed because it occurs in a past narrative:
She's **been working** all night. → When I got there, she **had been working** all night.
They've **been living** there for years. → They didn't like the house, even though they **had been living** there for years.
She's **been reading** for hours. → There were books everywhere – she **had been reading** for hours.

This is part of a newspaper story written in 1971. Rewrite it, putting the verbs into the *past perfect* or *past simple*. Start your story with the words:
By 1971, Mr and Mrs Charlton had been living in 17 Portland Street for five years. They had tried to move several times, but . . .

Mr and Mrs Charlton have been living in 17 Portland Street for five years. They have tried to move several times, but this has not been possible, as they are unable to sell their house. Several people have looked at the property, but quickly lost interest – and the reason for this is obvious.

For the past three years the garden of 17 Portland Street has been covered by three feet of water. The Charltons tried to find the reason for this strange occurrence, but no one has been able to help.

The water level has been rising since 1968, and looks as though it will soon endanger the entire ground floor: the Charltons have been keeping the water back with sandbags, but of course this is only a temporary defence. Mrs Charlton says she has contacted the water authorities, the town council, even her local MP – but so far no one has been able to explain why their back garden has become a swimming pool for all the children in the neighbourhood.

52 ★★★
Present, Past, Present Perfect: check

Write the verbs in the correct tense:

1   She paid for her ticket and . . . . . (leave)
2   I closed the door quietly because he . . . . to sleep. (try)
3   How many times . . . . since he came to New York? (he call)
4   I . . . . about this for some time now. (know)
5   They . . . . television – their favourite programme is on at the moment. (watch)
6   I wanted to be the first to tell her the news, but I was too late. Someone . . . . her. (already tell)
7   The children are filthy. Where . . . .? (they be)
8   I'm going to bed. I . . . . for hours and I'm tired. (work)
9   I think she's the nicest person I . . . . . (meet)
10   Mary was cleaning the windscreen when she . . . . a crack in the glass. (notice)
11   I couldn't open the office door because someone . . . . it. (lock)
12   I agree: I . . . . you should apologize. (not think)
13   When I phoned her, she . . . . her homework. (do)
14   We . . . . for three-and-a-half hours when John finally arrived. (wait)
15   When I shouted, they . . . . off the roof and . . . . away. (jump/run)
16   Don't phone her just now. She . . . . to her boss. (talk)
17   Oh! You . . . . a shave! You look strange without a beard! (have)
18   I . . . . military service for eighteen months. This is my last month. (do)
19   We . . . . for about four hours when I realized that something was wrong with one of the tyres. (travel)
20   Mary will be ready soon. She . . . . a bath at the moment. (have)
21   Sorry, I . . . .: could you say that again, please? (not understand)
22   We . . . . in the café until the rain stopped, and then went home. (stay)
23   . . . . here before? (you be)
24   There was nobody at the office. Mr Brownlow . . . . the staff to go home. (tell)
25   I signed the register and . . . . upstairs to my room. (go)
26   He had been working in the garden, but he . . . . when he saw us. (stop)
27   I couldn't drive to work because Mary . . . . the car. (use)
28   How many times . . . . him since he went to Edinburgh? (you see)
29   Peter and Jane . . . .: I could hear them from my room. (argue)
30   I . . . . him since he started working here. (never trust)
31   I'm worried. Why . . . . yet? (they not arrive)
32   They're very angry. They . . . . to see you for the last two or three hours. (try)
33   I wanted to help with the washing-up, but they . . . . it. (already do)
34   It's the most comfortable car I . . . . . (ever drive)
35   Peter was cleaning the flat and John . . . . the dinner. (make)
36   I had a pleasant surprise when I got to my room: someone . . . . some flowers there for me. (put)
37   . . . . that we should tell him tomorrow? (you agree)
38   They couldn't leave the studio when I called because they . . . . . (film)

39 I .... the machine for some time when I realized that there was no ink in it. (use)
40 When he warned them about the police, they .... the country. (leave)
41 Don't make a noise: the children .... to sleep. (try)
42 Oh! You .... a new dress! (buy)
43 She .... here for several years – four or five now, I think. (work)
44 We .... in the sunshine for about twenty-five minutes when I suddenly felt sick. (sit)
45 He'll be ready in a moment. He .... his shoes. (clean)
46 I .... listening to their complaints all day. One of these days I'll tell them what I really think. (hate)
47 I .... down on the bed and fell asleep. (lie)
48 I think I .... him somewhere before. (see)
49 I couldn't get into the car, because the children .... the car keys. (hide)
50 Peter was meeting someone that night, so I .... at the office and .... for a few hours. (stay/work)

The future tense

53 ☒
Present Continuous + time word

FORM

Present continuous (⇨ exercise 27) + time word (**tomorrow**, **next week**, **on Saturday**, **in two weeks**, etc):

I'm seeing them	on⎫ this⎭ Saturday in three days in two weeks' time this week/Friday next week/Friday

USE

● To talk about plans which are arranged for a particular time in the future. This construction is used very often with **come** and **go**, and with verbs like **see**, **stay**, **visit**, **meet**, etc:

They're going tomorrow.

I'm arriving next week.

We're visiting the States in three weeks.

NOTES

* Remember that a time word or expression must be used, or understood from the conversation, to make the *present continuous* a future.

* This is not just a 'near' future – it is possible to say:
  He's coming back in ten years.

Write these sentences in full, putting the verbs into the *present continuous* and supplying the missing words where necessary:

1   I / see / them / Saturday.
    I'm seeing them on Saturday.
2   They / come / here / three weeks.
    They're coming here in three weeks.
3   I / meet / John / three o'clock.
4   What / you do / Friday night?
5   I / go / to the disco / Saturday evening.
6   We / go back / to the States / three years.
7   They / go on holiday / two days' time.
8   I / not come home / Friday.
9   You / work late / tomorrow night?
10 We / not go to school / next week.
11 He / come to see you / tomorrow.
12 Mr and Mrs Green / go away / three weeks.
13 We / have a party / Saturday.
14 I / see her again / next week.
15 You / play football / this week?

54 ⊠
going to

FORM

Positive		
I	am ('m)	
He She It	is ('s)	going to pay.
We You They	are ('re)	

Question		
Am	I	
Is	he she it	going to pay?
Are	we you they	

Negative		
I	am not ('m not)	
He She It	is not (isn't) ('s not)	going to pay
We You They	are not (aren't) ('re not)	

USE

● To talk about a planned future action:
  *I'm **going to** see my parents on Saturday.*
  (This use is similar to *present continuous* + time word ⇨ exercise 53.)

- To talk about something in the future which we can see as a result of something happening now:
  *Look at those clouds. It's **going to** rain.*
  *That man on the bike is **going to** fall off!*

- To make statements about the future in a neutral way:
  *Alan's **going to** finish his exams on Friday.*
  *Jenny's **going to** be five next week.*
  *I'm **going to** work for a television company.*
  (The *future simple* is also used for this purpose ⇨ exercise 56.)

54a Write the correct form of **going to** to complete these sentences:

1 When (you) .... phone her?
   When are you going to phone her?
2 (They not) .... stay very long.
   They aren't going to stay very long.
3 What (you) .... say to your father?
4 (I not) .... pay anything.
5 (We) .... play tennis tomorrow?
6 (She) .... live in Mexico for a few months.
7 (The machine) .... work?
8 (Your parents) .... have a holiday this year?
9 (They) .... borrow some money from the bank.
10 (I not) .... eat there again.

54b Write the correct form of **going to** and use one of these verbs to complete the sentences. Use each verb once only:

finish	complain
fall off	be
miss	die
rain	drive
work	fail

1 Look at those clouds! It .....
   Look at those clouds! It's going to rain.
2 Look at the sun! It .... hot today.
3 Susan's not working very hard. I think she .... her exams.
4 He's very angry. He .... to the manager.
5 It's nearly four o'clock. The lesson .... soon.
6 I don't like travelling by plane. I .....
7 The machine's broken. It (not) .....
8 The President's very ill. I think he .....
9 Watch the baby! She .... the bed!
10 This bus is very slow. I think we .... the train.

55 ☒
going to / Present Continuous + time word

CONTRAST

- It is often possible to use either tense:
  I'm **seeing** them tomorrow.
  I'm **going to see** them tomorrow.

- The **going to** future is very common, especially in conversation.
  If there is doubt about which of the two futures to use, it is better
  to use **going to**.

- *Present continuous* + time word is generally used for plans arranged
  for a particular time in the future.

Supply the *going to* or *present continuous future* for these sentences. If two
answers are possible, write them both:

1 We .... at home tonight. (stay)
   We're going to stay at home tonight.
   We're staying at home tonight.
2 Look at the sky. It .... tomorrow. (rain)
   Look at the sky. It's going to rain tomorrow.
3 We .... at a restaurant tonight. (eat)
4 They .... to Manchester tomorrow morning. (drive)
5 I .... my teeth, have a wash, and go to bed. (brush)
6 Be careful with that plate! You .... it! (break)
7 My parents .... with us for a few weeks. (stay)
8 Who's .... him the news? (tell)
9 Hurry up! We .... the train! (miss)
10 How many people .... today? (arrive)

56 ☒☒
Future Simple

FORM

Positive			Question				Negative		
I He She It We You They	Will ('ll)	stay.	Shall/Will	I	stay?		I He She It We You They	will not (won't)	stay.
			Will	he she it					
			Shall/Will	we					
			Will	you they					

*   Note the negative contraction – **won't**.

*   **shall** is not used very often now. We generally use it only as a first person question (= with **I** or **we**) to make suggestions and offers:
Shall I carry your suitcase for you?
Shall we go to a restaurant?

USE:

●   For a statement of future fact. This can be
    a) certain:
      *The train **will be** half an hour late.*
      *The journey **will take** six hours.*
    b) uncertain:
      *I think it'**ll rain** tomorrow.*
      *I'm not sure he'**ll be** there.*
    Going to can also be used for this purpose ⇨ exercise 54.

●   For a sudden decision to do something (usually used with **I** or **we**):
    *No one's offered to help? I'**ll do** it for you!*
    *Wait a minute – I'**ll open** the door for you.*
    *I think I'**ll have** eggs and chips, please.*

●   To show willingness to do or not do something in the future (often as a promise or a threat):
    *I promise I'**ll be** there.*
    *I'**ll** never **speak** to him again.*

*He says he'**ll send** the money.*

⇨   exercise 79 for *future simple* in *conditional* sentences.

⇨   exercise 59 for *future simple* + **when**, **as soon as**, etc. ·

Write these sentences in full, putting the verbs into the *future simple:*

1   I'm sure he (not be) late.
    I'm sure he won't be late.
2   (I open) the window for you?
    Shall I open the window for you?
3   How long (the journey take?)
4   I suppose (she be) in London next week.

5 John (phone) your office for you.
6 (There be) a lot of people at the meeting?
7 What time (the race start?)
8 He (never agree) to your idea.
9 You (never see) your money again.
10 What's the matter? (I phone) the doctor?
11 Don't worry. I (pay) for the damage to your car.
12 (You be) at home tomorrow?
13 The company (not give) you an extra day's holiday.
14 Don't touch that! You (hurt) yourself!
15 There (not be) any newspapers tomorrow.

57 ★★

going to – future plan, and **will** – sudden decision

CONTRAST

● In conversation, **going to** is often used to indicate a future plan that has been made before the time of speaking:
  I'm **going to see** Pat tomorrow – we arranged it this morning.

● **Will** is often used to indicate a sudden decision, made at the time of speaking:
  How can we get to the airport? I know! I'**ll borrow** Sue's car!

Write the correct form of **going to** or **will** to complete the dialogue:

PAT: What are you doing this weekend, Jan?
JAN: I (see) a new play tomorrow at the Royal Court Theatre – 'Short Sharp Shock'.
PAT: Have you got the tickets yet?
JAN: No, I (get) them this afternoon, actually. Would you like to come?
PAT: Oh, thank you, that would be nice.
JAN: OK, I (get) you a ticket, too.
PAT: Great . . . what time does it start?
JAN: Eight o'clock, but we (all meet) in the Green Café at 7.15 . . .
PAT: OK, I (meet) you in the café, but, er . . . I (be) there about half-past seven.
JAN: That's fine.
PAT: Oh, one other thing . . . I've got no money at the moment . . . I (pay) for the ticket on Saturday. Is that OK?
JAN: Yes, that's OK, no problem.
PAT: (You eat) in the café, or just have a cup of coffee?
JAN: Just a coffee, I think . . .
PAT: Look, (we go) to a restaurant after the show? I know a very good Chinese restaurant. . .
JAN: That's a good idea – I (phone) the others and see if they want to come too.
PAT: Good, and then I (book) a table . . . Great! I (see) you tomorrow.
JAN: Yes, see you . . . bye!

58 ★★
going to and **will**

CONTRAST

● Sometimes it is possible to use either **going to** or **will**, but at other times only one of them is correct:

going to	1 future plan – decided before time of speaking	ex 57	I'm going to leave next week.
	2 future result from present evidence	ex 54	He's going to fall off his bike.
will	1 future willingness	ex 56	I won't do it.
	2 sudden decision made at time of speaking	ex 57	I'll phone her now.
	3 offer/suggestion	ex 56	Shall I open the door for you?
going to or **will**	1 neutral future fact[1]	ex 54 ex 56	I think it's going to rain tomorrow. I think it'll rain tomorrow.
	2 first conditional[2]	ex 79	If it rains we're going to leave. If it rains we'll leave.
	3 **when/as soon as**, etc[2]	ex 59	I'm going to phone when I arrive. I'll phone when I arrive.

[1] **will** is more common here.
[2] **will** or **going to** can be used, according to context.

Write the correct form of **going to**, **shall**, or **will**, for these sentences. If two answers are possible, write the more likely one:

1   'Why is Sheila getting a passport?'
    'She . . . . live in Spain for a year.'
    '*She's going to live in Spain for a year.*'
2   I know she . . . . (not) agree with this idea.
    I know she won't agree with this idea.
3   I think the film . . . . be a big success.
    I think the film will be a big success.
    I think the film is going to be a big success.
4   'I don't feel very well this morning.'
    'Oh, dear . . . . I look after the children for you?'
5   The managing director . . . . sack two hundred people next month.
6   'There's someone at the door.' 'OK, I . . . . answer it.'
7   She . . . . never see her parents again.
8   'Is that your new stereo?'
    'Yes, but it doesn't work. I . . . . to take it back to the shop.'
9   'You light the fire, and I . . . . cook some food.'
10 I think the exam . . . . be quite easy.
11 'I see Mary and Peter together a lot.' 'Yes. They . . . . get married.'
12 You . . . . probably have a really good time.
13 What are your plans? (You) . . . . see your parents this weekend?

14   The dog looks ill. I think it . . . . be sick.
15   What (you) . . . . this weekend?
16   I . . . . see a late-night horror film at the Odeon.
17   You don't have to walk: I . . . . give you a lift.
18   I've had enough of this job. I . . . . leave.
19   Of course we . . . . help you.

59 ⭐⭐
when + Present Simple to describe the future

FORM

when +	present simple,	future simple
When As soon as Before After If / Unless	I see him,	I'll phone you.

USE

● The present simple is used in clauses of time and condition (after **when**, **as soon as**, **if**, etc) to refer to the future.

● **until** is similar:

future simple +	**until** +	present simple
I'll wait	until	I see him.

NOTES

*   Note the use of the *present simple* above:
    (NOT ~~When I'll see him I'll phone you.~~)
    (NOT ~~I'll wait until I'll see him.~~)

*   The *present perfect* can also be used with **when**, etc:
    I'll speak to you when I've finished.

*   **Going to** or the *imperative* can be used, when necessary, instead of the *future simple*:
    I've decided what to do. I'm going to talk to him when he gets here.
    Phone me when he arrives.

Write these sentences, putting the verbs into the *future simple* or *present simple*:

1   I (give) it to them when they (visit) us.
    I'll give it to them when they visit us.
2   I (not send) the parcel until I (hear) from you.
    I won't send the parcel until I hear from you.
3   As soon as they (phone) me I (contact) you.

4 I (see) you before I (fly) to Paris.
5 They (send) you the money before they (leave).
6 When I (talk) to him I (give) him your news.
7 She (visit) her parents before she (go) to the airport.
8 I (finish) this when I (be) at the office.
9 I (send) you a postcard when I (get) to Bermuda.
10 She (do) her homework before she (go) out.
11 After I (visit) the hospital, I (go) and see her parents.
12 I (phone) Mary when we (get) to San Francisco.
13 I (call) you as soon as we (sign) the contract.
14 He (not do) anything before you (tell) him to.
15 You (be) very surprised when you (meet) him.
16 I (talk) to you when the game (be) over.
17 When she (hear) this she (be) very pleased.
18 You probably (not like) him when you (meet) him.
19 As soon as I (hear) the results I (let) you know.
20 When they (find out) about this there (be) trouble.

60 ★★★
Present Simple as future

'What time does our train leave?'
'The train leaves at eight, we arrive at Dover at twelve,
and get on the ferry an hour later.'

USE

● To describe an organized future timetable.

Do these sentences refer to the *habitual present* or the *future*? Write P or F
in your notebooks next to each question number:

1 I leave home at eight, walk to the station, and catch the 8.30 train. I
   always get to the office before nine. (*P*)
2 The committee leaves Stockholm on Sunday morning, arrives in
   Australia on Monday and starts work on Tuesday. (*F*)
3 Your plane leaves London at 8.30 and arrives in Cairo at 12.00.
4 I travel by the 8.30 train because it gets to London before ten o'clock.
5 You take the 1.30 train from Berlin which connects with the night ferry
   from the Hook of Holland. You arrive in London an hour before your
   appointment.

6   I always take the night train from Edinburgh which arrives in London at half-past six.

7   The hovercraft leaves Felixstowe at 12.00. It takes an hour, so you get there at 14.00 French time.

8   The Prime Minister arrives in India on Tuesday, spends a couple of days in Delhi, then goes on to Malaysia.

9   The local train is very slow and stops at all the stations between here and Peterborough.

10   The bus leaves at four o'clock, we get to Dublin at seven, and we have to register at the hotel before half-past eight.

61 ★★★
Future Continuous

FORM

Positive				*Question*				*Negative*		
I He She It We You They	will ('ll)	be working.		Will	I he she it we you they	be working?		I He She It We You They	will not (won't)	be working.

USE

● To describe an action or event that will be in progress at some time in the future:
  I'll be waiting at the station when you arrive.
  I'll be watching the football at six.

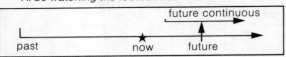

● To describe an activity or state that covers the whole of a future time period:
  I'll be watching television all evening.
  I'll be living in London for the next few weeks.

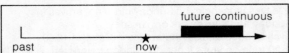

● To describe a future event which has already been arranged or is part of a regular routine.

I'll be seeing him tomorrow – I'll give him your note.
I'll be working at home tomorrow – you can call me there.

NOTES

*   **going to** or *present continuous* + time word can frequently be used
    instead of the *future continuous*. The main difference between the
    three is that **going to** and *present continuous* + time word usually refer
    to planned or intentional futures:

    ***I'm going to see** her tomorrow – we arranged it last week.*
    ***I'm seeing** her tomorrow, to talk about the new contract.*
    and the *future continuous* is less intentional:
    ***I'll be seeing** her tomorrow at the weekly sales conference: I'll talk to
    her about it then.*

*   *Future continuous* is sometimes used to refer to the present, when we
    are guessing about what people are doing:

    *Peter and Tom **will be lying** on the beach in Corfu at the moment . . .*
    *I bet they'**ll be having** a good time now that it's hot.*
    *They'**ll** probably **be staying** at an expensive hotel somewhere.*

Write the verbs below as *future continuous* or *future simple*. If two answers
are possible, write them both:

1   I (see) them tomorrow – I (tell) them what you said.
    I'll be seeing them tomorrow – I'll tell them what you said.
2   (You work) all tomorrow evening?
    Will you be working all tomorrow evening?
3   She (stay) in Leeds all weekend.
4   She (visit) our office next week – I (ask) her then.
5   I (see) the sales manager at the marketing meeting on Monday and I'm
    sure she (give) me the figures then.
6   I (not be able) to lend you the car tomorrow – I (use) it all night.
7   Next year they (live) in Spain.
8   This time next week we (sit) on the beach.
9   The children (stay) with their grandparents for the summer holidays.
10 At four o'clock on Tuesday afternoon we (fly) over Paris.
11 What (you do) early on Monday night?
12 They (come) round for dinner tomorrow evening – I (show) them the
    photographs then.
13 What time (the train arrive) tomorrow night?
14 We (not hear) from him for some time – he (be) in Panama.
15 I (not do) any work at all during the holidays.

62 ★★★
Future Perfect

FORM

Simple:

| **will/'ll** + **have** + *past participle* |

Positive

| I
He
She
It
We
You
They | will
('ll) | have gone
by 4 o'clock. |

Question

| Will | I
he
she
it
we
you
they | have gone
by 4 o'clock? |

Negative

| I
He
She
It
We
You
They | will not
(won't) | have gone
by 4 o'clock. |

Continuous:

| **will/'ll** + **have been** + *verb -ing* |

Positive

| I
He
She
It
We
You
They | will
('ll) | have been
working here
for 3 years
in January. |

Question

| Will | I
he
she
it
we
you
they | have been
working here
for 3 years
in January. |

Negative

| I
He
She
It
We
You
They | will not
(won't) | have been
working here
for 3 years
in January. |

USE

- *Simple* – to look ahead to a time in the future when:
  a) an expected event or activity will be in the past:
  I'll have finished work by five o'clock tonight.

  b) a duration of time will be in the past:
  I'll have been here for a year in January.

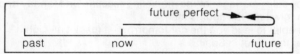

- *Continuous:*
  a) with **for** or **since**, to describe a period of time which precedes a point in the future:
  We'll have been living here for two years by July.
  (This can also be *future perfect simple* – see b) above)

  b) to describe an activity which leads up to a point in the future:
  I'll be dirty because I'll have been playing football.

Write the verbs below in the *future perfect simple* or *continuous*. If two answers are possible, write the answer which you think is best for the sentence:

1   They'll probably be hungry because they . . . . . (not eat)
    They'll probably be hungry because they won't have eaten.
2   I'll be tired tonight because I . . . . all day. (work)
    I'll be tired tonight because I'll have been working all day.
3   I . . . . the entire committee by the time I leave England. (meet)
4   I . . . . for seven years when I get my degree. (study)
5   We . . . . here for six months by the time they find us a new flat. (live)
6   I . . . . for forty-five years by 1990. (work)
7   They . . . . in the cold for six hours by the time we pick them up. (stand)
8   Another million people . . . . unemployed by this time next year. (become)
9   She . . . . Prime Minister for ten years by 1991. (be)
10 They . . . . for five hours by eight o'clock. (play)
11 We . . . . for two days by the time we get there. (drive)
12 They . . . . for twenty-four hours by twelve o'clock tomorrow. (not eat)
13 When they've talked to me, the police . . . . everybody in the office.
    (question)
14 She . . . . a member of the committee for twenty-five years by the time
    she retires. (be)

63 ★★★
The future: check

Write the following sentences in the correct form (*present continuous*, *present simple*, *going to*, *future simple*, *future continuous*, *future perfect simple*, or *future perfect continuous*). If more than one answer is possible, write the most likely one:

1   We've run out of milk.'
    'Oh, have we? I . . . . and get some.' (go)
    'Oh, have we? I'll go and get some.'
2   'So you've bought your new house – Congratulations!'
    'Thank you – we . . . . a party when we . . . . in.' (have/move)
    'Thank you – we're going to have a party when we move in.'
3   I'm afraid I can't come to dinner on Saturday – I . . . . Tim. (meet)
4   Ronald . . . . five next Tuesday. (be)
5   It's raining, so we . . . . take an umbrella. (have to)
6   Next November we . . . . married for fifteen years. (be)
7   I . . . . you know when Mary . . . . . (let/phone)
8   Just think ! This time next week we . . . . on the beach! (lie)
9   I . . . . at the airport when your plane . . . . . (wait/land)
10 In two weeks' time she . . . . her exams. (finish)
11 '. . . . Brian at the meeting?' (you see)
    'No – he . . . . on holiday next week.' (be)
12 We . . . . when Jane . . . . here. (go/get)
13 At ten o'clock I . . . . for sixteen hours. (drive)

64 ★★★
Future in the past

FORM

> **was/were going to** + *infinitive*
> *I was going to leave early, but I didn't.*

USE

● To describe a planned future action that did not happen:

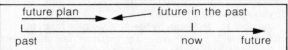

*I **was going to visit** my parents yesterday, but my car broke down.*
*He **was going to say** something, but changed his mind.*
*They **were going to stay** in the Grand Hotel, but it was full – so they stayed with us instead.*

NOTES

* *Future in the past* can also be expressed by the construction **I thought I would**, **She thought she would**, etc + *infinitive*:
*I always **thought I'd** be a musician.*
*They **thought they would** stay in the Grand Hotel, but it was full – so they stayed with us.*

The first column describes what Jan planned to do: the second describes what actually happened. Write how he describes his life, using one sentence for each number:

Plans	**Reality**
1 Go to university.	1 Failed exams. Left school at sixteen.
2 Find a job in Madrid.	2 No jobs. Decided to go to England to study English.
3 Study English in London.	3 Didn't like London. Went to Cambridge instead.
4 Stay with an English family.	4 Changed my mind. Stayed in a student hostel.
5 Study English for two years.	5 Didn't have enough money. Finished after eighteen months.
6 Work in England when I finish at school.	6 Couldn't find a job. Came back to Madrid.
7 Not going to work in my parents' restaurant.	7 Needed the money. I did.

1   *I was going to go to university, but I failed my exams, so I left school at sixteen.*

Simple, continuous, and perfect aspects

65 [★★★]
Tense check

Copy this table into your notebook and give an example of the positive, question, and negative of each tense:

	Tense	Verb	Positive	Question	Negative
1	Present Simple	she/agree	She agrees	Does she agree?	She doesn't agree
2	Present Continuous	he/leave	He's leaving		
3	Past Simple	they/leave			
4	Past Continuous	he/shout			
5	Present Perfect Simple	they/arrive			
6	Present Perfect Continuous	she/work			
7	Past Perfect Simple	they/go			
8	Past Perfect Continuous	they/sleep			
9	Future Simple	he/leave			
10	Future Continuous	they/work/ tomorrow			
11	Future Perfect Simple	they/leave/ by tomorrow			
12	Future Perfect Continuous	they/work/ all day			

⇨ exercises 53–64 for other future tenses.

66 [★★★]
Simple and Continuous Aspects

The *tense* of a verb tells us that it is *present*, *past*, or *future*: the *aspect* gives us other information. There are three aspects – *simple*, *continuous*, and *perfect*.

The simple aspect refers to the whole of an activity or event, and not just part of it:

I'**ll have** a bath tonight. (future simple)
I **worked** from eight o'clock to ten. (past simple)
I **go** to the office by car. (present simple)

It is used to describe:
● a general truth:
   Big cars use a lot of petrol.

- a repeated, habitual action:
  Classes start at nine o'clock.
- a complete event or series of events:
  We went to Spain for our holiday.
- feelings, perceptions, etc – i.e. any verb that is not an 'activity' verb:
  I understood the lecture quite well.

The continuous aspect describes an event (or series of events) at some point between its beginning and its end. It is used with activity verbs – e.g. **play**, **run**, **walk**, **go**, **move**, **drive**, etc – and it is the activity which is important, rather than the end result:

> They**'re working** at the moment. *(present continuous)*
> I **was reading** when you phoned. *(past continuous)*
> At this time tomorrow we'**ll be saying** goodbye. *(future continuous)*

It is used to describe:

- an activity in progress:
  I was working in the garden when she called.
- a repeated action which is temporary, and viewed at some time between the beginning and end of the temporary period:
  I'm cycling to work this week because my car's in the garage.
- a temporary situation viewed at some point between its beginning and its end:
  I'm living in London at the moment.

Choose between the *simple* and *continuous aspect* in the following sentences. If two answers are possible, write them both:

1 'Where's Stella?'
  'She (play) tennis in the park.' (present)
  'She's playing tennis in the park.'
2 They (go) abroad three times last year. (past)
3 I (see) you outside the cinema at eight o'clock. (future)
4 The telephone (ring) but I (watch) my favourite programme so I (not answer) it. (past)
5 Simon (work) really hard for his exams next month. (present)
6 He (live) away from home when he starts college. (future)
7 Cats (not like) water. (present)
8 I (not understand) what she (mean) at first, but then she (explain) more clearly. (past)
9 I think I (make) a cup of tea. (future)
10 The bottle (roll) off the table and (smash) when it (hit) the floor. (past)
11 I (call) at the office but they (all work) so I (not stay) long. (past)
12 I (see) my parents tonight so I (give) them your message then. (future)
13 I (not understand) a single word he (say). (present)
14 Five or six people (wait) to see Mrs Blackstone. (present)
15 The bottle (roll) off the table, but I (catch) it before it (go) over the edge. (past)

67 ★★★
Perfect Aspect

The *perfect aspect* can be either *simple* or *continuous*. It tells us:
- that the activity or state being discussed occurs or starts before a certain point in time: and
- that the activity or state has an important connection with that later point in time:

 I **have been** to France twice. (*present perfect*: the events occurred before the present time – now)

 It was 1946. The war **had finished** *and Jack* **had left** *the army.* (*past perfect:* the events occurred before the past time – 1946)

 Come tomorrow at 7.30. I' **ll have had** *dinner by then.* (*future perfect:* **dinner** will occur before a future time – tomorrow at 7.30)

Write the sentences below, putting the verbs into the *present perfect*, *past perfect*, or *future perfect*, and using the simple or continuous forms:

1 (You see) that film yet?
   Have you seen that film yet?
2 I (write) letters all day, and I'm tired.
   I've been writing letters all day, and I'm tired.
3 I (not play) football since I was at school.
4 How long (you wait) to see the doctor?
5 They (talk), but they stopped when I came into the room.
6 By the end of this month, I (work) here for ten years.
7 When I arrived, the party (finish).
8 We've got two more hours. We (do) all the housework by the time your parents arrive.
9 I (read) that book for two months but I (not finish) it yet.
10 They (wait) for me for two hours when I finally arrived.
11 We (know) each other since we were at school together.
12 They (try) to solve the problem for some time now.
13 The machines (work) continuously for two years when they get their first service next month.
14 We (work) on the car for two hours before it finally started.
15 By tomorrow, they (get) permission to have the meeting at the town hall, I'm sure.
16 (anyone arrive) when you got to the office?
17 She looks very tired – I think she (do) too much overtime.
18 I (not see) her for the last five years.
19 (You say) goodnight to the children yet?
20 When I got there, I could see that they (not expect) me.

Verb formations

68 ★★
Irregular verbs: check

Irregular verbs are usually listed in three different columns:

Infinitive	Past Simple	Past Participle
be	was	been
have	had	had
go	went	gone

68a Copy these tables into your notebook and add the missing words:

Infinitive	Past Simple	Past Participle	Infinitive	Past Simple	Past Participle
be	was	been			driven
beat	beat	beaten			eaten
	became			fell	
		begun	feel		
	bent			fought	
	blew				found
		broken		flew	
	brought		forget		
build			forgive		
burn				got	
	burst				given
		bought		went	
	caught		grow		
choose				heard	
come					hidden
	cost		hit		
		cut	hold		
do			hurt		
draw			keep		
dream				knew	
	drank		learn		

Infinitive	Past Simple	Past Participle	Infinitive	Past Simple	Past Participle
	left			shot	
		lent			shown
	let			shut	
lie			sing		
light			sit		
lose				slept	
	made				spoken
	meant			spent	
meet			stand		
	paid			stole	
		put			swum
	read			took	
ride			teach		
	ran		tell		
		said	think		
	saw			threw	
sell					understood
send				wore	
	set		win		
shine				wrote	

68b Complete these sentences, putting the verbs given into the *past simple* or *present perfect*. If two answers are possible, write the more likely one:

1 They . . . . us at football for the last five years. (beat)
   They have beaten us at football for the last five years.
2 She . . . . manager of the factory in 1982. (become)
   She became manager of the factory in 1982.
3 We . . . . the meeting yesterday at 3.30 p.m. (begin)
4 The wind . . . . hard all through last night. (blow)
5 I'm sorry – I . . . . one of your glasses. (just break)
6 . . . . your books back already? (they bring)
7 I . . . . my fingers on a hot plate when I was making the dinner. (burn)
8 We . . . . a new house last week. (buy)
9 The police . . . . the person who stole my purse. He's at the police station now. (catch)
10 We . . . . the new person for the job. (already choose)
11 Nobody . . . . to see me yesterday. (come)

12 It was very expensive – it . . . . a thousand dollars. (cost)
13 I . . . . the cake into four pieces and took it into the sitting room. (cut)
14 . . . . the washing-up yet? (you not do?)
15 The bottle's empty – someone . . . . all the milk. (drink)
16 We . . . . for hours before we arrived. (drive)
17 I . . . . for two days, and then I had some soup. (not eat)
18 Someone . . . . into the swimming pool. (just fall)
19 I . . . . terrible when I woke up this morning. (feel)
20 I . . . . some money in the street last night. (find)

68c Complete these sentences, putting the verbs given into the *present perfect* or *past simple*. If two answers are possible, write the more likely one:

21 . . . . in an aeroplane before? (you ever fly)
22 . . . . what I told you to do? (you already forget)
23 They . . . . to the airport at eight o'clock. (get)
24 My parents . . . . me some money when I left home. (give)
25 There's nobody here – everybody . . . . out. (go)
26 He . . . . the news yet. (not hear)
27 She was so angry that she . . . . him. (hit)
28 . . . . when you left the dentist? (your mouth hurt)
29 I asked them to be quiet, but they . . . . talking. (keep)
30 I . . . . him since we were at school together. (know)
31 I . . . . a lot since I started coming to this school. (learn)
32 How many people . . . . the factory since the new manager arrived? (leave)
33 I . . . . him £500. (already lend)
34 The police . . . . me talk to Jane after she was arrested. (let)
35 We . . . . the beds and cleaned the rooms. (already make)
36 . . . . the taxi-driver yet? (you pay)
37 I carried the suitcases into the hall and . . . . them by the front door. (put)
38 She . . . . most of his books already. (read)
39 I left the house and . . . . quickly down the street. (run)
40 He was very angry, and . . . . something which wasn't very polite. (say)

68d Complete these sentences, putting the verbs given into the *present perfect* or *past simple*. If two answers are possible, write the more likely one:

41 I . . . . the doctor about it, but she couldn't help. (already see)
42 I'm sorry, the car's not here – I . . . . it. (just sell)
43 She . . . . you a letter three weeks ago. (send)
44 He gave me a cup of tea and . . . . me his stamp collection. (show)
45 I . . . . the door quietly when I left. (shut)
46 She . . . . very well, but I didn't like the band. (sing)
47 They . . . . down and started eating. (sit)
48 I was so tired I . . . . for twelve hours. (sleep)

49 . . . . to John's teacher about his homework yet? (you speak)
50 I'm afraid I . . . . all my money. (already spend)
51 I . . . . in the rain and waited for the bus. (stand)
52 She dived into the sea and . . . . for about half an hour. (swim)
53 . . . . my photograph yet? (you not take)
54 She . . . . in this school since 1984. (teach)
55 Someone . . . . me about your new job. (just tell)
56 I can't answer your question – I . . . . about it yet. (not think)
57 She . . . . the ball to me and I caught it. (throw)
58 I . . . . what he was trying to say, but Pat didn't. (understand)
59 She . . . . expensive clothes and drove a Mercedes. (wear)
60 I . . . . sixty letters asking for jobs. (already write)

69 ★★★
Irregular verbs: further practice

Write the missing words for these irregular verbs:

Infinitive	Past Simple	Past Participle	Infinitive	Past Simple	Past Participle
bet	bet	bet	leap		
bite			mistake		
bleed			rise		
cling			sew		
creep			shake		
dig			shrink		
feed			sink		
flee			slide		
freeze			tear		
lead			weep		

70 ★★★
Verbs taking gerund, infinitive, or indirect speech

● Some verbs are followed by the *infinitive*:
  *She advised me **to go***.

● Some verbs use the *gerund*:
  *I like **driving***.

● Some verbs use *indirect speech*:
  *They complained **that they had been waiting for hours***.

● Certain verbs can use all three.
   *We agreed **to go**.*
   *We agreed **that we should go**.*
   *We agreed **about going**.*

* Note that exercise 70c combines the answers from 70a and 70b in a
   table. Both exercises show constructions commonly following the verbs
   given; sometimes the verb is followed by more than one construction.
   Phrasal verbs (e.g. **ask after**, **finish off**, etc) are not included, neither
   are less common constructions or prepositions.

70a Make sentences using the constructions given. Put the verbs into the
past simple tense:

1　(accuse of + gerund)
　　They . . . . me / take the money.
　　They accused me of taking the money.
2　(advise + **to**–infinitive)
　　She . . . . me /wait.
　　She advised me to wait.
　　(advise + gerund)
　　She . . . . wait / for a while.
　　She advised waiting for a while.
　　(advise + **that**–indirect speech)
　　She . . . . / they / wait.
　　She advised that they should wait.
3　(agree + **to**–infinitive; agree on/ about + gerund; agree + **that**–indirect
　　speech)
　　We . . . . / leave early.
　　We agreed to leave early.
　　We agreed on/about leaving early.
　　We agreed that we should leave early.
4　(apologize for + gerund)
　　I . . . . / be late.
　　I apologized for being late.
5　(ask + **to**–infinitive; ask + **if**–indirect speech)
　　Peter . . . . / speak to Janice.
　　Peter asked to speak to Janice.
　　Peter asked if he could speak to Janice.
6　(begin + **to**–infinitive; begin + gerund)
　　We . . . . / read the instructions.
7　(believe in + gerund; believe + **that**–indirect speech)
　　We . . . . / tell the truth.
8　(complain about + gerund; complain + **that**–indirect speech)
　　They . . . . / be hungry.
9　(continue + **to**–infinitive; continue + gerund)
　　Mary . . . . / work at home.
10　(decide + **to**–infinitive; decide + **that**–indirect speech; decide
　　on + gerund)
　　We all . . . . / have a picnic.

11 (dream + **that**–indirect speech; dream of/about + gerund)
    I . . . . / fly to the moon.
12 (encourage + **to**–infinitive)
    They . . . . / me / practise every day.
13 (enjoy + gerund)
    He . . . . / swim a lot.
14 (expect + **to**–infinitive; expect + **that**–indirect speech)
    She . . . . / go to Paris for the summer.
15 (finish + gerund)
    They . . . . / eat at ten.
16 (forget + **to**-infinitive; forget about + gerund; forget + **that**–indirect
    speech)
    I . . . . / phone my mother.
17 (hate + gerund; hate + **to**–infinitive)
    She . . . . / be bored.

70b Decide if the following sentences can be finished correctly by A, B,
    and/or C. Sometimes all three are possible:
18 (help) We all helped
    A to move the car. B moving the car. C that the car moved.
    Answer: *A*
19 (hope) I had hoped
    A to be able to come soon. B for coming soon.
    C that I'd be able to come soon.
    Answer: *A* and *C*
20 (insist) They insist
    A to see the manager. B on seeing the manager.
    C that they should see the manager.
21 (intend) I intend
    A to stay here for some time. B staying here for some time.
    C that I should stay here for some time.
22 (invite) We invited them
    A to come to the party. B for coming to the party.
    C that they should come to the party.
23 (know) They already knew
    A to leave. B about leaving early. C that they should leave early.
24 (learn) John soon learned
    A to work the machine. B about working the machine.
    C that he should work the machine.
25 (let) Why didn't they let
    A him go? B him going? C that he should go?
26 (love) The children love
    A to play with Mark. B playing with Mark.
    C that they should play with Mark.
27 (make) They made
    A him stay. B him staying. C that he should stay.
28 (manage) We finally managed
    A to open the car door. B opening the car door.
    C that we opened the car door.

29 (mind) Do you mind
   A me to smoke? B my smoking? C if I smoke?
30 (miss) I miss
   A to live near my family. B living near my family.
   C that I don't live near my family.
31 (offer) They offered
   A to pay for the damage. B paying for the damage.
   C that they would pay for the damage.
32 (order) He ordered
   A them to stay there. B them staying there.
   C that they should stay there.
33 (plan) We planned
   A to arrive at nine o'clock. B on arriving at nine o'clock.
   C that we should arrive at nine o'clock.
34 (prefer) I prefer
   A to work alone. B working alone. C that I should work alone.
35 (promise) They promised
   A to visit her. B about visiting her. C that they would visit her.
36 (recommend) I would recommend
   A you to have the seafood. B having the seafood.
   C that you have the seafood.
37 (refuse) They refused
   A to leave. B leaving. C that they would leave.
38 (remember) I remembered
   A to pick up my keys. B picking up my keys.
   C that I had picked up my keys.
39 (seem) You seem
   A to be tired. B being tired. C that you are tired.
40 (start) After an hour, we started
   A to work more slowly. B working more slowly.
   C that we worked more slowly.
41 (stop) Some time later, they stopped
   A to rest. B working. C that they should rest.
42 (suggest) She suggested
   A to go to a different school. B going to a different school.
   C that we should go to a different school.
43 (think) I thought
   A to go abroad. B of/about going abroad. C that I would go abroad.
44 (tell) They told me
   A to leave early. B about leaving early. C that I should leave early.
45 (try) Please try
   A to speak more quietly. B speaking more quietly.
   C that you should speak more quietly.
46 (want) Do you want
   A to go home? B going home? C that you should go home?
47 (warn) I warned him
   A to be careful. B against driving too fast.
   C that he shouldn't drive too fast.

70c Copy the following table into your notebook, and fill it in according to the answers you have given in the last forty-seven sentences. If the gerund is preceded by a particular preposition, write the preposition in the box:

	Infinitive	Gerund	Indirect Speech		Infinitive	Gerund	Indirect Speech
accuse		√ of		let			
advise	√	√	√	love			
agree	√	√ on about	√	make			
apologize		√ for		manage			
ask				mind			
begin				encourage			
believe				miss			
complain				offer			
continue				order			
decide				plan			
dream				prefer			
encourage				promise			
enjoy				recommend			
expect				refuse			
finish				remember			
forget				seem			
hate				start			
help				stop			
hope				suggest			
insist				think			
intend				tell			
invite				try			
know				want			
learn				warn			

*   Note that **seem** can be followed by **that** when used with **it**:
It seems that they aren't coming.

The passive

71 ☒
The passive: Present Simple and Past Simple

FORM

> | noun/pronoun + | **to be** + | past participle |
> |---|---|---|
> | It | **was** | stolen. |
> | The televisions | **are** | made in Japan. |

USE

● *The passive* is used to describe actions:
  a) when we don't know who does, or did, the action:
  My briefcase was stolen last night.
  (I don't know *who* stole it).
  b) when it is not important to know who does, or did, the action:
  The cars are taken to Europe every week.
  (It doesn't matter *who* takes them).
  These televisions are made in Japan.
  (It doesn't matter *who* makes them).

My briefcase was stolen last night.

Rewrite these sentences putting the verb in the *passive*:

1   My car / damage / last night. (past)
    My car was damaged last night.
2   This computer / make / in the USA. (present)
    This computer is made in the USA.
3   The machines / make / in Scotland. (present)
4   The President / kill / last night. (past)
5   The money / change into dollars / at the bank. (present)
6   The parcel / post / yesterday. (past)
7   Cheese / make / from milk. (present)
8   The children / give / some food. (past)
9   The house / paint / every year. (present)
10 Several people / be hurt / in an accident last night. (past)

72 ☒☒
The passive: Present Simple, Past Simple, Present Perfect
Simple

● Passive sentences describe what happens to people or things, often as
  a result of action by other people or things:
  a) *The house has been painted.*
  b) *Mary was arrested yesterday by the police.*

• Passive sentences indicate that what happens is more important than who is responsible. For example, in the active sentence:
  c) *Simon has painted the house.*
  the speaker is talking about Simon and the house. In the passive sentence a), the house alone is being discussed. Similarly, in sentence b), the important news is about Mary, not about the police.

FORM

Present	*noun/pronoun* + **is/are**	+ *past participle*
	The cars are	taken abroad.
Past	*noun/pronoun* + **was/were**	+ *past participle*
	The cars were	taken abroad.
Present Perfect	*noun/pronoun* + **has/have been**	+ *past participle*
	The cars have been	taken abroad.

• The rules for choice of tense are the same in *the passive* as they are for active sentences, i.e. if a verb should be *present perfect* in the active form, it will be the same tense in *the passive*.

⇨ exercise 73 for *passives* in all tenses.

Rewrite these verbs as *passives*, keeping them in the same tense, and removing **they**, **we**, **someone**, etc:

1 We clean the garages every day.
   The garages are cleaned every day.
2 Someone has given him a lot of money.
   He has been given a lot of money.
3 The police arrested two hundred people.
   Two hundred people were arrested.
4 We check every car engine thoroughly.
5 We export this computer to seventy different countries.
6 They have cancelled the meeting.
7 We opened the factory at nine o'clock.
8 They send two million books to America every year.
9 We have invited all the students in the school.
10 We have told him not to be late again.
11 They posted all the letters yesterday.
12 The machine wraps the bread automatically.
13 They paid me a lot of money to do the job.
14 Fortunately, they didn't damage the machinery.
15 We send the newspapers to Scotland by train.

73 ★★★
The passive: all tenses, simple and continuous

FORM

Present	*Simple:*	**is/are** + *past participle*
		The letters are delivered here.
	Continuous:	**is/are being** + *past participle*
		He's being interviewed at the moment.

Past	*Simple:*	**was/were** + *past participle*
		They were sent by train.
	Continuous:	**is/were being** + *past participle*
		My suit was being cleaned at the time.

Present Perfect	*Simple:*	**has/have been** + *past participle*
		All the tickets have been sold.
	Continuous:	—

Past Perfect	*Simple:*	**had been** + *past participle*
		I was too late: the papers had been removed.
	Continuous:	—

Future	*Simple:*	**will be** + *past participle*
		You will be met at the station.
	Continuous:	—

Infinitive	**(to) be** + *past participle*
	I don't want to be arrested.
	We shouldn't be arrested.

USE

⇨ exercises 71 and 72. Choice of tense is the same as for active sentences.

NOTES

*   The *passive* is frequently used to describe scientific or mechanical processes, or in formal explanations:
    *The passive **is** frequently **used** . . .*

*   It is not essential to repeat the auxiliary verb **to be** in a list of processes:
    The cars are washed, cleaned, checked, and then driven to the ports.

73a Copy this passage into your notebook and underline all the passives:

Acid rain <u>is caused</u> by burning coal or oil. When either fuel <u>is burned,</u> it releases poisonous gases which <u>are carried</u> up into the atmosphere and sometimes <u>transported</u> long distances.

Over 3,000 research projects have been carried out to look into acid rain, and a decision to tackle the problem has been taken in most of the western European countries. Measures have been taken in Scandinavia and in Central Europe to stop the pollution before it is dumped on the environment: and a diplomatic campaign has been launched to convince other countries that the problem has to be considered as a major ecological threat.

'Five years ago this issue was not being treated seriously,' says one leading environmental group, 'but now that damage has been reported in large areas of forest and lakeland, our politicians are being forced to take action. This problem must be solved quickly: if governments do nothing, they will be faced in two or three years' time with the accusation that they have allowed our forests to die.' A major international initiative to combat acid rain is expected in the near future.

73b Rewrite these sentences in the same tense as the original, using the words given. The subject of the active sentence can often be omitted; you should include it in the passive sentence only if it is necessary:

1   Someone's interviewing Dr Johnson at the moment.
    Dr Johnson . . . .
    Dr Johnson's being interviewed at the moment.
2   You mustn't use this machine after 5.30 p.m.
    This machine . . . .
    This machine mustn't be used after 5.30 p.m.
3   We had warned him the day before not to go too near the canal.
    He . . . .
4   They were painting the outside of the ship when the accident happened.
    The outside of the ship . . . .
5   You must clean this machine every time you use it.
    This machine . . . .
6   You should keep the flowers in a warm sunny place.
    The flowers . . . .
7   They're mending your shoes at the moment.
    Your shoes . . . .
8   Someone will drive your car to Edinburgh on Tuesday.
    Your car . . . .
9   We don't allow smoking in this restaurant.
    Smoking . . . .
10 You should pay your bill before you leave the hotel.
    Your bill . . . .

11 I have told the children about the party.
    The children . . . .
12 About thirty million people are watching this programme.
    This programme : . . . .
13 We expect students not to talk during the examination.
    Students . . . .
14 You mustn't touch this button while the experiment is in progress.
    This button . . . .
15 Someone will blow a whistle if there is an emergency.
    A whistle . . . .
16 Someone was carrying the bomb to a safe place when it exploded.
    The bomb . . . .
17 Someone's moved my chair!
    My chair . . . .
18 The police are questioning Mr and Mrs Davidson.
    Mr and Mrs Davidson . . . .
19 Someone checks the water level every week.
    The water level . . . .
20 We invited two hundred people to the wedding.
    Two hundred people . . . .

74 ★★
To have something done
FORM

---

subject +	**has/have**	+ *object* +	*past participle*
James	has	his car	cleaned every week.

USE

● To describe an action which I (or you, he, she, etc) arrange but do not
  do myself:
  I had my suit cleaned last week.
  She's going to have her house repaired by the Council.

NOTES

∗ All tenses are possible:
  I*'m having* my house painted at the moment. (present continuous)
  I*'ve had* the car fixed. (present perfect)
  I*'ll have* your coat cleaned for you. (future)

∗ Note the word order. The *object* goes before the *past participle* – there
  is a difference between:
  He had his car cleaned. and *He had cleaned his car.*

∗ **Get** can be used in the same way as **have**:
  She's going to get her house repaired by the Council.

*   Note the colloquial use:
    I had my bag stolen last week.
    This is not an arranged action.

Rewrite these sentences using **have** + *object* + *past participle*, changing
some words if necessary:

1   Someone delivers the newspapers. (We)
    We have the newspapers delivered.
2   Someone cleaned the carpets every year. (I)
    I had the carpets cleaned every year.
3   Their house needs painting. (They're going to)
    They're going to have their house painted.
4   We ask someone to check the accounts every month. (We have)
5   Someone sends the money to my bank account in London. (I have)
6   My stereo isn't working properly. It needs cleaning. (I'm going to)
7   My camera's being repaired at the moment. (I'm having)
8   He spilt coffee on my jacket – so he took it away for cleaning. (He spilt
    coffee on my jacket – so he)
9   I think it's time to service the car. (It's time to)
10 I don't like the office curtains. It's time to change them. (I think I'll)
11 There's something wrong with the typewriter. It needs repairing. (I think
    I'll)
12 We couldn't go to Jack's flat: it was being painted. (We couldn't go to
    Jack's flat: he)
13 The computer's no good: we're changing it. (We're having)
14 I send the films to England: they are processed there. (I have)
15 I didn't want to eat in the hotel dining-room, so I asked them to send a
    meal up to my room. (I didn't want to eat in the hotel dining-room, so I)

Miscellaneous

75 ★★★
wish

●   **wish** can be followed by several different tenses. The three most
    important are **wish** + *past simple*, **wish** + *past perfect*, and
    wish + **would** + *infinitive*.

a) **wish** + past simple

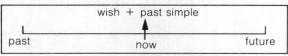

I wish things were different now.

This expresses an unrealistic desire for the present situation to be different. The desire is unrealistic because there is very little chance of the change occurring.

FORM

subject + **wish** + *past simple*		
I	wish	I was rich.
I	wish	I lived in America.
Do you	wish	we lived nearer the school?

I wish I was rich.

* This *past simple* can have a special form with the verb **to be**: **were** instead of **was** (in formal or written English). So we can say:

   *I wish I **were** rich.* or *I wish I **was** rich.*
   *He wishes he **were** rich.* or *He wishes he **was** rich.*

75a Rewrite these sentences using **I wish** + *past simple:*

1 I'd love to live in Australia.
   I wish I lived in Australia.
2 I hate having to go to school on Saturdays.
   I wish I didn't have to go to school on Saturdays.
3 Why don't we go abroad for our holidays?
4 I'd love to be a film star.
5 Why don't we have a bigger house?
6 I'd love to speak more languages.
7 I'd love to be able to cook.
8 Why is the school so expensive?
9 I never have enough money: it would be nice to have more.
10 I hate having to do homework every night.

b) **wish** + past perfect

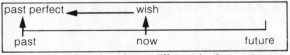

I wish things had been different in the past.

This expresses a desire that an action or event in the past had been different.

FORM

subject + **wish** + subject + past perfect		
I	wish	I	hadn't stolen that money.
I	wish	she	had come to my party.

75b Rewrite these sentences using **I wish** + past perfect:

1 I decided to work in London.
  I wish I hadn't decided to work in London.
2 We sold the house we had in Manchester.
  I wish we hadn't sold the house we had in Manchester.
3 We went to live with my parents in Surrey.
4 I decided to stop working as a bus driver.
5 We put our money into a grocery shop.
6 We borrowed £3,000 to start the business.
7 We didn't realize that a supermarket was opening nearby.
8 The grocery shop closed down.
9 We lost all our money.
10 It was a mistake to leave Manchester.

I wish I hadn't stolen that money.

c) **wish** + **would** + infinitive

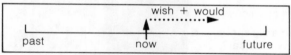

I wish things would change soon.

This expresses annoyance with a person or situation and a desire for a situation to change, either now or in the future. The change could possibly occur, but we do not expect it to. It generally depends on action from some other person or thing.

FORM

subject + **wish** + subject + **would** + infinitive			
I	wish	he	would	give up smoking.
I	wish	it	would	stop raining.
I	wish	she	would	be more careful.

* **would** can be shortened to **'d**:
  *I wish she**'d** be more careful.*
* Note the difference between this and the **'d** (= **had**) in the past perfect:
  *I wish she**'d** been more careful.*

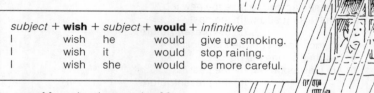

I wish it would stop raining.

75c Mr and Mrs Reynolds are worried about their children. Write what they want them to do, using **I wish** + **would**:

1   John never comes home before twelve o'clock.
     I wish John would come home before twelve o'clock.
2   Susan isn't working very hard for her exams.
     I wish Susan would work harder for her exams.
3   Peter doesn't wash very often.
4   Sheila isn't very polite to her grandparents.
5   John doesn't help with the housework.
6   I'd like Peter to give up smoking.
7   Sheila takes too many days off work.
8   I don't like John playing football all the time.
9   Sheila and Susan are very unkind to Peter.
10   John doesn't wear a tie very often.

NOTES

*   **if only** can be used instead of **wish** in all three constructions described
     above. It is stronger and more unrealistic than **wish**:
     If only I was rich.
     If only I hadn't stolen that money.
     If only it would stop raining.

76 ★★★
wish: check

76a Answer the questions:

1   I wish I had a big car.
     a) Do I have a big car?
     b) Am I talking about (i) the present?
                            (ii) the past?
     Answers: a) *No* b) (i) *the present*
2   I wish I'd gone to university.
     a) Did I go to university?
     b) Am I talking about (i) the present?
                            (ii) the past?
3   If only she'd take the new job.
     a) Has she agreed to take the new job?
     b) Am I talking about (i) the past?
                            (ii) the present/future?
4   I wish they hadn't phoned the police.
     a) Did they phone the police?
     b) Am I talking about (i) the past?
                            (ii) the present/future?
5   I wish she spoke French.
     a) Can she speak French?
     b) Did she speak French?
     c) Are we talking about (i) the past?
                              (ii) the present?

6   I wish she would speak French.
    a) Can she speak French?
    b) Is she speaking French?
    c) Are we talking about (i) the past?
                            (ii) the present/future?
7   I wish I could agree with you.
    a) Do I agree with you?
    b) Am I going to change my mind?
    c) Am I talking about (i) the past?
                          (ii) the present?
8   If only he'd agreed with us.
    a) Did he agree with us?
    b) Am I talking about (i) the present?
                          (ii) the past?

76b Write these sentences, choosing the correct verb tenses:

1   I wish it (stopped / would stop) raining.
    I wish it would stop raining.
2   I wish it (hadn't snowed / wouldn't snow) yesterday.
    I wish it hadn't snowed yesterday.
3   I wish (I knew / I'd know) the answer to your question.
4   I wish you (wouldn't be / aren't) so rude.
5   I wish (they visited / they'd visited) us when they were in town.
6   I wish (I'd speak / I spoke) better French.
7   I wish they (hadn't been / wouldn't have been) so unfriendly.
8   I wish (I've refused / I'd refused) when you suggested the idea.
9   I wish (I had / would have) more time to do this job.
10 I wish she (would / had) come to work on time in future.

77 ★★
used to

●   **used to** is a tense indicating something that happened regularly in the
    past but doesn't happen now:
    *I **used to** smoke.* (= I don't smoke now)
    *She **used to** work for the BBC.* (= she doesn't work for the BBC now)
    *He **didn't use to** like me.* (= he likes me now)

FORM

	used to +	*infinitive*
She	used to	live here.
I	used to	smoke.

NOTES

*   The negative is **didn't use to** + *infinitive*
    She didn't use to smoke.

* The question form is **did** + *subject* + **use to** + *infinitive*?
  Did you use to live here?

* The question and negative forms are not used very often.

77a Write these sentences, putting one verb into the correct form of **used to** and the other into the *past simple*:

1 I (smoke), but I (give it up) last year.
   I used to smoke, but I gave it up last year.

2 I (not like) him, but then I (change) my mind.
   I didn't use to like him, but then I changed my mind.

3 He (live) in London before he (go) abroad.

4 I (earn) a lot of money, but then I (lose) my job.

5 I'm surprised that they (join) the tennis club. They (not like) tennis.

6 (you travel) a lot before you (get) this job?

7 I (work) in a factory before I (become) a teacher.

8 She (drive) a lot before she (have) the accident.

9 That old radio (work) before I (drop) it.

10 We (see) them every week, but then we (have) an argument.

11 I (work) in a restaurant before I (go) to college.

12 She (play) a lot of tennis before she (break) her leg.

13 We (have) a garden, but then we (move) to a different house.

14 She (live) in Wales, but then she (move) back to Scotland.

15 I (drive) a lorry before I (start) this business.

77b There is another construction: **I'm used to** + *gerund*: **to be used to** doing something = to be in the habit of, to be accustomed to:
*I'm used to work**ing** at night.* (= working at night is a normal activity for me)

* Note the difference in meaning:
  I'm used to working at night. (= it is normal for me to do this)
  I used to work at night. (= I often worked at night, some time ago)

Write these sentences, choosing the correct form of **used to** or **be used to**:

1 (I'm used to / I used to) live in London, but I moved.
   I used to live in London, but I moved.

2 (They're used to / They used to) cooking for themselves when they get home from school.
   They're used to cooking for themselves when they get home from school.

3 Do you remember how (we used to / we're used to) listen to music all the time?

4 (Were you used to / Did you use to) spend hours in front of the mirror when you were young?

5 (I'm not used to / I didn't use to) eating this sort of food.

6 (This is used to / This used to) be an industrial area.

7 (I'm used to / I used to) earn more when I was a teenager than I do now.

8 The children (didn't use to / aren't used to) going to bed so late.
9 (I'm not used to / I didn't use to) driving on the left.
10 (I used to / I'm used to) walk to work when I was younger.
11 (I didn't use to / I wasn't used to) like classical music.
12 (I'm not used to / I didn't use to) getting up so early.
13 (I didn't use to / I wasn't used to) having so much exercise.
14 (They used to / They were used to) take the children to school for us before their car broke down.
15 (We're used to / We used to) see each other every day.

78 ☒
The imperative

USE

● To give orders and instructions:
Stop!
Don't go!
Turn left at the traffic lights and then *turn right*.

FORM

● The *imperative* has the same form as the *infinitive*:
Wait!
Negative is formed by adding **don't**:
Don't wait!
Don't stop!

NOTES

* The *imperative* is used to give instructions in the second person, i.e. *(You) wait!* The form is the same for the singular and the plural.

   Let's is a kind of *imperative* for **we**:
   Let's go.
   Let's not wait. (Note the negative)

* The *imperative* is not always very polite. It is more polite to say **Could I have** . . . or **Would you** . . .
   Give me some bread → *Could I have* some bread, please?
   Open the door ———→ *Would you open* the door, please?

* The *imperative* may sometimes be used for requests to people we know well, or for orders given by people in authority. It is often used when speaking to children or soldiers.

Mr and Mrs Brownridge are talking to their children, Jo and Pat. In your notebooks, write what they say under their thoughts:

1 The door's closed. Pat can open it.

2 Jo's going to touch the cooker. It's hot.

3 I don't want Pat to be late tonight.

Open the door, Pat!

Don't touch the cooker, Jo!

4 I need to lift this box. Pat can help me do it.

5 It's time for Jo to get up.

6 I want Pat to bring me an ashtray.

7 I want Jo to be quiet.

8 The window's closed: it's hot. Pat's there.

9 I'd like Pat to turn down her stereo.

10 I'd like Jo to pass the salt.

Conditionals

There are three main types of conditional. These are usually described as the First, Second and Third Conditionals.

79 ★★
The First Conditional

FORM

if + *present simple*	*future*
If you drop it,	it'll break.
If you come at ten,	we'll be ready.
If you phone me,	I'll pick you up at the park.

or *future*	***if*** + *present simple*
It'll break	if you drop it.
We'll be ready	if you come at ten.
I'll pick you up later	if you phone me.

USE

● The *first conditional* refers to the future. It is used when there is a possibility that the **if**-event might happen.

If it rains, we'll go to the cinema. (= It might rain: it might not)
If the sun shines, we'll go to the beach. (= The sun might shine: it might not)

* **going to** is sometimes used in the *first conditional* to describe a future plan:
If it rains, we're going to visit my mother.

Write these sentences, putting the verbs in brackets into the *present simple* or the *future simple*:.

1   If the train's late, we (walk).
    If the train's late, we'll walk.
2   She (call) you if she (have) time.
    She'll call you if she has time.
3   If it costs too much, I (buy) a smaller one.
4   If the doctor can't see me, I (go) somewhere else.
5   If the class (be) full, we (find) another one.
6   What will we do if the taxi (not come)?

7 Will you phone me if there (be) any problems?
8 I (ask) Peter if I (see) him tomorrow.
9 I (go) next week, if I (can) get a train ticket.
10 If I (have) to, I (complain) to the manager.
11 If he (see) me here, he (be) really angry.
12 Mary (be) worried if you don't come to the airport.
13 If it (snow) this winter, we (go) skiing.
14 I (lend) them some money if they (ask) me.
15 If you (visit) Oxford, you (see) some interesting old buildings.

80 ★★
The Second Conditional

FORM

if + past simple·	*would*/*could*/*might* + infinitive
If I lived by the sea,	I would do a lot of swimming.
If they asked me to work for them,	I might accept.

or *would*/*could*/*might* + infinitive	*if* + past simple
I would do a lot of swimming	if I lived by the sea.
I might accept	if they asked me to work for them.

*   The 'past' here is actually the *subjunctive*, which is the same as the *past simple* except for two forms – **I** and **he/she** + **to be**:
    If I were you, I'd change my job.
    If John were here, he wouldn't be very happy.

*   In conversational English, these two forms can be replaced by the past:
    If I was you, I'd change my job.
    If John was here, he wouldn't be very happy.

*   **would** is often shortened to **'d**.

USE

● The *second conditional* refers to the present or future.
   The **if**-event is either

   a) hypothetical:
       If I worked in that factory, I'd soon change things. (but I don't work in that factory)
       If I spoke French, my job would be a lot easier. (but I don't speak French)

   b) unlikely:
       If she left her husband, she might be happier. (but I think she's not going to leave her husband)

Write these sentences putting the verbs in the sentences below into the correct tense:

1 If you drove more carefully, you (not have) so many accidents.
   If you drove more carefully, you wouldn't have so many accidents.
2 If he (get up) earlier, he'd get to work on time.
   If he got up earlier, he'd get to work on time.
3 If we (have) more time, I could tell you more about it.
4 If you (sell) more products, you'd earn more money.
5 I could help you if you (trust) me more.
6 His car would be a lot safer if he (buy) some new tyres.
7 The children would be better swimmers if they (go) swimming more frequently.
8 I wouldn't mind having children if we (live) in the country.
9 If I (be) you, I wouldn't worry about going to university.
10 If I (have) any money, I'd give you some.
11 Your parents (be) a lot happier if you phoned them more often.
12 Where would you like to live if you (not live) in Paris?
13 What would you do if you suddenly (win) half a million pounds?
14 Would you mind if I (not give) you the money I owe you today?
15 If I had to go to hospital, I (not go) to this one.

81 ★★
First and Second Conditional: check

CONTRAST

Some students get confused by the difference between the *first* and *second conditional*. Look at these two sentences:
a) *If she works harder, she'll pass her exams.*
b) *If she worked harder, she'd pass her exams.*
The difference between the two sentences can be found by asking the question, 'Is she going to work harder?' In sentence a) the answer is, 'Maybe – and maybe not'. The answer to sentence b) is, 'Probably not'. The difference is the idea in the speaker's mind of what is going to happen. The **if**-event in a *first conditional* sentence is more likely to happen than the **if**-event in a *second conditional*.

Choose the correct answer to the questions below:

1 'If Mary found out what was happening, she'd be very angry.'
   Is Mary going to find out what's happening?
   A Maybe   B Probably not
   Answer: *B*
2 'If Mary finds out what's happening, she'll be very angry.'
   Is Mary going to find out what's happening?
   A Maybe   B Probably not
3 'If they sacked him, the factory would go on strike.'
   Are they going to sack him?
   A Maybe   B Probably not

4   'If they sack him, the factory will go on strike.'
    Are they going to sack him?
    A Maybe   B Probably not
5   'What would you do if someone told us to leave?'
    Is someone going to tell us to leave?
    A Maybe   B Probably not
6   'What will you do if someone tells us to leave?'
    Is someone going to tell us to leave?
    A Maybe   B Probably not
7   'If they don't agree with me, I'll go to the director.'
    Are they going to agree with me?
    A Maybe not   B Probably not
8   'If they didn't agree with me, I'd go to the director.'
    Do they usually agree with me?
    A Maybe   B Yes   C No
9   'If I don't like your ideas, I'll say so.'
    Am I going to like your ideas?
    A Maybe not   B Probably
10 'If I didn't like your ideas, I'd say so.'
    Do I usually like your ideas?
    A Maybe   B Yes   C No

82 ★★★
The Third Conditional

FORM

> **if** + past perfect   **would/could/might** + perfect infinitive
> If I had met you earlier, I wouldn't have married Jo.
> If I'd worked harder, I would have passed the exam.
>
> or **would/could/might** + perfect infinitive   **if** + past perfect
> I wouldn't have married Jo if I'd met you earlier.
> I would have passed the exam if I'd worked harder.

USE

● The *third conditional* refers to the past (it is sometimes called the *past conditional*):
   I'd have warned you if I'd seen you last week. (but I didn't see you, so I didn't warn you)
   If I'd passed my exams I would have gone to Art College. (but I didn't pass my exams, so I didn't go to Art College)

Write these sentences in full, using the words given. You will need to add some words, and put the verbs into the correct tense:

1   What / would / you / done / if / I / not / lend / you / the money?
    What would you have done if I hadn't lent you the money?

2   If / you / asked / me for tickets / I / could / get / you some.
   If you had asked me for tickets I could have got you some.
3   I / not / marry / him / if / I / know / what he was like.
4   I / not / hire / a car / if / I / know / how expensive it was.
5   If / we / got / to the cinema earlier / we / not / miss / the start of the film.
6   If / I / be born / a year earlier / I / have to do / military service.
7   If / you / asked / me / I / would lend / you my car.
8   If / I gone / to university / I / get / a better job.
9   I / wouldn't / go out / yesterday / if / you asked / me not to.
10 I / could / give you / a lift / if / my car / not broken down.
11 I / not go / to Berlin / if / I know / what was going to happen.
12 I would / stay / longer / if / she / wanted me to.
13 I / not come / to this school / if / I / know / what it was like.
14 We / would go / to his party / if / we / able to / find a baby-sitter.
15 I / visit / you / in hospital / if / I / know / you were there.

83 ★★★
'Zero' Conditional

There is another conditional which is often called *zero conditional*.

FORM

> ***if*** + *present simple*   *present simple*
> If you press the button,   the machine switches off.
> If you go in the best seats, you get a free drink.
>
> or *present simple*   ***if*** + *present simple*
>   The machine switches off   if you press this button.
>   You get a free drink   if you go in the best seats.

USE

- **If** has the same meaning as **when** here.
   The *zero conditional* is used:

   a) for instructions:
      If you select reverse gear, the car goes backwards.
      If the camera is on, a red light appears.

   b) for general truths:
      If he's got no money, he doesn't go out.
      He always says hello if he sees you.

Put the verbs into the correct tense:

1   Water (freeze) if the temperature falls below zero.
   Water freezes if the temperature falls below zero.
2   If he's angry, his face always (go) bright red.

3   If you put your money in a savings account, you (get) ten per cent interest.
4   If the microphone isn't working, you (can not) hear what he's saying.
5   The radio (not work) if the batteries are flat.
6   If there (be) only a few students, we usually close one of the classes.
7   The machine (not work) if it (not have) enough oil.
8   If a balloon is filled with hot air, it (rise).
9   If water (boil), it (change) into steam.
10 The machine (stop) automatically if something (go) wrong.

84 ★★★
Words other than **if**

● Other words can be used instead of **if** in conditional clauses:

   a) **unless** = 'if not':
      I'll go home soon if the film doesn't start.
      I'll go home soon unless the film starts.

   b) **provided (that)**, **on condition (that)**, **as long as**, **so long as**:
      Provided that everybody agrees, we'll have the meeting on Tuesday.

   c) **(just) suppose**, **supposing (that)**, **what if**, **imagine**:
      Just suppose it didn't rain for four months: would we have enough water?

The words are not always interchangeable. Their use depends on the context of the sentence.

Choose the correct word or words to replace the words in italic in these sentences:

1   'I'll give you £100 *if* you say nothing about this.' (provided that, what if, unless)
    'I'll give you £100 provided that you say nothing about this.'
2   '*If* your company went bankrupt, what would you do?' (just suppose, on condition, as long as)
3   '*If* you had to live in another country, where would you go?' (on condition, unless, imagine)
4   'We'll let him out of prison *if* he reports to the police station every day.' (supposing, as long as, unless)
5   'I'll take them to court *if* they *don't* pay me what they owe.' (imagine, provided that, unless)
6   '*If* you won a million pounds – what would you do with it?' (providing, as long as, unless, imagine)
7   '*If* they keep to the agreement, I'll give them the money.' (what if, imagine, so long as)
8   'You'll be alright *if* you take some travellers' cheques.' (provided that, imagine, what if)
9   'I'll complain to the manager *if* you *don't* give me a different room.' (as long as, unless, imagine)

10   '*If* all the hotels were full, where would we stay?' (provided that, as long as, suppose)

85 ★★★
Sentences containing hidden conditions

● *Conditional* sentences are sometimes long and complicated, and they are not always fully expressed in conversation – especially where the *if*-event has already been mentioned, or can be understood from the context of the conversation:

'*James didn't come to the party.*'
'*What a pity. I'm sure he would have enjoyed it.*'

The second statement depends on the hidden condition 'if he had come':

I'm sure he would have enjoyed it (if he had come).

● Other examples of hidden conditions:

'*Be careful, Tom. I wouldn't hurry this decision.*' (if I were you)
'*You should have come. You would have loved it.*' (if you had come)

Copy these two conversations into your notebook and underline the sentences containing hidden conditions:

a)

MR ANDERSON: I don't think he should go.

MRS ANDERSON: Why not? He's sixteen, he's old enough. I'm sure he wouldn't do anything stupid.

MR ANDERSON: You know him – he'd get involved in a fight. I don't think he could look after himself. He'd get hurt!

MRS ANDERSON: I'm sure he'd keep out of trouble.

MR ANDERSON: Are you? Well, I'm not. I don't think we should let him go.

b)

MARTHA: I think we should go to Scotland for the holiday. I'm fed up with going abroad and getting sick. We'd enjoy ourselves more in Scotland.

JAMES: Oh, I don't think so. The weather's terrible up there. We wouldn't be able to sunbathe or go swimming, there'd be nothing to do.

MARTHA: We could go walking in the mountains. That would be lovely.

JAMES: Well I think it would be dangerous. You know what terrible mists they have in Scotland. There are always stories about people getting lost in the mountains.

MARTHA: How about going with a group – the Youth Club, for instance?

JAMES: Oh, you know you'd hate that. You can't stand organized holidays . . .

86 ★★★
Mixed tense conditionals

Although conditionals are usually presented as *first*, *second* or *third conditionals* (⇨ exercises 79, 80 and 82), the *present simple* does not always have to go with the *future simple*, **would** does not always have to go with the *past simple*, etc:

If I'd stayed at school, I would be in university now. (past event with consequences in the present)
If you hear the alarm, get out as fast as you can. (general condition + *imperative*)
I'll take your plate if you've finished. (*future simple* offer dependent on *present perfect* event)
If he saw us, he always said hello. (*zero conditional* in past tense)

Match the two halves of the sentences and write them in your notebook: Example: *1* and *E* go together: *If he was happy, I was happy.*

1   If he was happy,
2   If you hadn't lost your job,
3   If she didn't lose her temper so quickly,
4   If she doesn't do her work,
5   Can I borrow your pen
6   If the machine stopped,
7   You wouldn't be so hungry
8   Whistle
9   If I study here for another month,
10 If it's raining,

A   we stopped.
B   she wouldn't have got into that fight.
C   I wouldn't go out for a walk.
D   I'll have been here for a year.
E   I was happy.
F   send her home.
G   if you'd eaten a proper breakfast.
H   we wouldn't be living here.
I   if you see the police coming.
J   if you've finished using it?

87 ★★★
The conditional: check

Write these sentences putting the verbs into the correct tense:

1   If you'd stayed at home, there (not be) any trouble.
    If you'd stayed at home, there wouldn't have been any trouble.
2   What would you do if he (resign) tomorrow?
    What would you do if he resigned tomorrow?

3   It's a pity John didn't come to the football. He (like) it.
     It's a pity John didn't come to the football. He would have liked it.
4   I'll do it if he (ask) me.
5   I wouldn't have been so upset if Judy (write) to me earlier.
6   If we offered him more money, (he stay) here?
7   If she's gone out, we (ask) Peter to do it for us.
8   I (look after) the children if you carry the suitcases.
9   We would have missed the train if we (be) two minutes later.
10   It's a pity Terry wasn't at the party. He (love) it.
11   Phone the police if you (see) anything strange.
12   I'm going to scream if you (not stop) playing that guitar.
13   The children always (get) frightened if they watch horror films.
14   (You let me know) what happens if I don't get to the meeting?
15   I don't know what I'd do if John (be) in an accident.
16   There (be) trouble if they try to stop him leaving.
17   Can I take the typewriter if you (finish) with it?
18   It's a pity David isn't here. He (be) very amused.
19   Shout if you (see) anything unusual.
20   If you (look after) the car, it will never break down.
21   If you (look after) the car, it wouldn't break down so much.
22   If you (look after) the car, we'd be able to sell it now.
23   Why didn't you watch my programme? You (enjoy) it.
24   If he weren't so bad-tempered, his wife (not leave) him so soon after
     the marriage.
25   (Ask) for help if you're having problems.
26   I (not go out) if I'd known he was so ill.
27   What (you say) if I offered you a job?
28   He (be) tired when we see him tomorrow if he's been working all night.
29   Tell me if there (be) anything wrong.
30   The engine starts if you (turn) this key.

➪ exercise 102 for a comparison of **could**, **would**, and **might**.

Modals

'Modals' are the small verbs like **can**, **must**, and **might**, which give certain meanings to main verbs.

FORM

There are twelve modal verbs:

can	shall	must
could	should	ought to
may	will	need (to)
might	would	dare

● *Positive* is formed by putting the modal between the subject and the main verb:

We should stay.
You ought to go.
He might come.

● *Negative* is formed by adding **not** (or **n't**) after the modal:

We shouldn't stay.
You ought not to come.
He might not come.

● *Questions* are formed by changing the position of the modal and the subject:

Should we stay?   *Shouldn't we stay?*
Ought you to go?   *Oughtn't you to go?*
Might he come?   *Mightn't he come?*

NOTES

*   **need** can be **needn't** (modal form) or **don't need to** (non-modal).

*   Negative questions generally use **n't**. If **not** is used, there is a different word order:
Should we not stay?

88 ⭐
Using modals in questions and negatives

Rewrite these sentences as *questions* or *negatives*, according to the instruction given:

1 I must go to the hospital tonight. (negative)
I mustn't go to the hospital tonight.
2 James can play the piano. (question)
Can James play the piano?
3 Peter can pay for us. (question)
4 We must go to the passport office today. (negative)
5 We can go to the bank tomorrow. (negative question)
6 You should phone the school today. (negative)
7 You can answer all the questions. (question)
8 She can pay for the lessons. (negative)
9 You can talk to Mary for me. (question)
10 Peter can check the times of the trains for us. (question)
11 We must say goodbye to Alan and Sue. (question)
12 They can stay here for a week. (negative)
13 We can buy a return ticket here. (question)
14 They should help you. (negative)
15 You can take the children home. (question)
16 He can understand me. (negative question)
17 He must stay at home today. (question)
18 You can show me the way to the theatre. (question)
19 We must give them the money. (question)
20 They can play football today. (negative question)

89 ⭐⭐
can, could

- **can**: (i) **know how to**, **be able to**:
  I can swim.
  Mary can speak French.

  can: (ii) **be allowed to**:
  You can sit here.
  My mother says I can't go out tonight.

- **could**: (i) past of **can**:
  I'm sorry, I couldn't come yesterday.
  I couldn't go to work this morning.

  could: (ii) used in second conditional (⟹ exercise 80)
  If you gave me the money, could I do the shopping?

- Requests: both **can** and **could** are used in requests. **Could** is more polite:
  Can I have a glass of water, please?
  Could you open the door for me, please?

NOTES

* **can** refers to the future if it is followed by a time word (**next week**, **tomorrow**, etc):

   I can do it for you next month.

* In the negative: **can** ⟶ **can't**, **cannot**, or **can not**.

   could → **couldn't**, or **could not**.

Complete these sentences using **can** or **could**. If two answers are possible, write them both:

1   . . . .n't you find John yesterday?
    Couldn't you find John yesterday?
2   . . . . I come and see you tomorrow?
    Can / Could I come and see you tomorrow?
3   . . . . you pass me the salt, please?
4   . . . . you play the guitar?
5   Why . . . .'t the children go to the cinema tonight?
6   . . . . you help me with my suitcase, please?
7   . . . . you drive my car if you had to?
8   . . . . you answer the phone for me?
9   Why . . . .'t you come to the disco tomorrow?
10 It was very difficult to hear: I . . . .n't understand what she was saying.
11 . . . . I smoke in here?
12 We had an appointment yesterday afternoon, but he . . . .n't see me.
13 I . . . . do the job for you next year.
14 . . . . you tell me the time, please?
15 I . . . .n't find my front door key last night.

90 ★★
can, could, be able to: tense changes

* **be able to** is used instead of **can** in the future, and sometimes also in the present and past:

Present	**can** or **am able to**
Past	**could** or **was able to**
Future	— **will be able to**

NOTES

* **can** sometimes indicates future when used with a time word (⟹ exercise 89).

* **be able to** is used in all tenses (**have been able to**, **had been able to**, etc).

* For **can't have** and **couldn't have** ⟹ exercises 100 and 101.

* In most cases, **could** and **was able to** have the same meaning.
  Sometimes, however, there is a small difference in meaning:
  *I **could** drive when I was sixteen, but I **wasn't able to** because I didn't
  have a licence.*
  could = ability, **was able to** = ability + action

Complete these sentences using the correct form of **can**, **could**, or **be able
to**. If two answers are possible, write the more likely one:

1 I'll . . . . see you tomorrow.
   I'll be able to see you tomorrow.
2 It was too expensive – I . . . . buy it.
   It was too expensive – I couldn't buy it.
   It was too expensive – I wasn't able to buy it.
3 . . . . I have a word with you, please?
4 . . . . you . . . . come out with us today?
5 . . . . you help me carry this downstairs?
6 Will she . . . . come to the office tomorrow?
7 I tried to see her, but I . . . . .
8 It was so heavy that I . . . . lift it.
9 I . . . . come tomorrow, I'm afraid. I'm too busy.
10 . . . . you . . . . contact your parents yesterday?
11 He . . . . (not) work since his illness.
12 After a few hours, I . . . . open the door and get out.
13 I . . . . see you next Monday at ten.
14 They didn't come to the restaurant – they . . . . (not) afford it.
15 When they came back from Paris they . . . . speak perfect French.

91 ★★
must, have to: positive and negative

● **must** and **have to** have similar meanings in the *positive*:
  You must leave. (= you can't stay)
  You have to leave. (= you can't stay)

● **must** and **have to** have different meanings in the *negative*:
  You mustn't leave. (= obligation – you can't go)
  You don't have to leave. (= no obligation – you can go or stay, as you
  like)

NOTES

* **have to** is not a modal verb. It is included in this section because it
  often has the same meaning as **must**, and is used instead of **must** in
  some tenses (⇨ exercise 92). It forms questions and negatives in the
  same way as all other main verbs.

* **have got to** has the same meaning as **have to**:
  I've got to go. = I have to go.

Match the pairs of sentences which are closest in meaning:
Example: *1* and *7* are similar in meaning.

1   You have to leave.
2   You don't have to leave.
3   You mustn't leave.
4   Must you go?
5   You don't have to take the job.
6   You mustn't take the job.
7   You must go.
8   You mustn't take the money.
9   You don't have to take the money.
10   You can stay if you like.
11   You can decide whether to take the job or not.
12   You have to stay.
13   Do you have to go?
14   You definitely shouldn't take the job.
15   Don't take the money.
16   You can take the money or leave it, as you like.

92 ★★
must, **have to**: tense changes

● **have to** is used instead of **must** in *future* and *past* tenses, and
sometimes in the *present*:

Present	**must** or **have to**
Past	— **had to**
Present Perfect	— **have had to**
Future	— **will have to**

NOTES

*   **have to** can be used in all tenses.

*   **must** sometimes indicates future when used with a time word:
     I must do this tomorrow morning.

*   For **must have** ⇨ exercises 100 and 101.

*   Note the different forms for *questions* and *negatives*:
     You must leave.   I have to go now.
     You mustn't leave.   I don't have to go now.
     Must you leave?   Do I have to go now?

*   For the difference in meaning between **mustn't** and **don't have to** ⇨
     exercise 91.

Put the correct form of **must** or **have to** in these sentences. Use the negative or question if necessary and put **have to** in the correct tense. If two answers are possible, write the most likely one:

1 I . . . . leave the party early last night – I wasn't very well.
   I had to leave the party early last night – I wasn't very well.
2 I'm sorry, you . . . . smoke in here.
   I'm sorry, you mustn't smoke in here.
3 The children are happy because they . . . . do any homework today.
4 You . . . . get up early tomorrow if you want to catch the bus.
5 . . . . (you) have a visa to come here?
6 It was a very bad accident. You . . . . be more careful in future.
7 He's been ill. He . . . . stay in bed since last month.
8 I've told the children that they . . . . come home before ten on Saturday nights.
9 . . . . (you) do military service in your country when you were young?
10 It was a lovely holiday. We . . . . do anything.
11 They were very rude. They . . . . apologize the next day.
12 The teacher told us that we . . . . work harder.
13 You . . . . get a passport before you go abroad next month.
14 We . . . . come back by boat because the airport was closed by fog.
15 You . . . . borrow my books without asking.

93 ★★
should, ought to

● **should** and **ought to** have similar meanings. **ought to** always uses **to**, **should** never uses **to**:
   Should we go?
   Ought we to go?
   You shouldn't make a noise in here.
   You oughtn't to make a noise in here.

NOTES

* **should / ought to** are not as strong as **must / have to**:
   You must go now! (= you have no choice: go now)
   You should go now. (= it's your decision, but if I were you I would go now)

* Note the position of **to** in **ought to**:
   You ought to go home now.
   You oughtn't to go home now.
   Oughtn't you to go home now?

* **should** is used more often than **ought to**.

Complete these sentences, using **should** or **ought to** and the words given:

1 It's past the children's bedtime. (they / be / in bed)
   They should be in bed.
   They ought to be in bed.

2   Can't they see the 'No Smoking' sign? (they / not smoke / in here)
     They shouldn't smoke in here.
     They oughtn't to smoke in here.
3   These windows are dirty. (you / clean them / more often)
4   Peter drives too fast. (he / drive / more carefully)
5   He owes you a lot of money. (you / not lend him / any more)
6   There won't be much food at the party. (we / take something / to eat?)
7   I'm not sure what to wear at the wedding. (I / wear / a suit?)
8   He says he can get us what we want. (we / pay him / now?)
9   The hotel is too expensive. (we / not stay / here)
10   It's their wedding anniversary next week. (maybe we / send them / a
     present)

94 ★★★
should, ought to, must, have to

●   Advice or recommendation: **should** and **ought to** have similar
    meanings (⇨ exercise 93):
    You should tell your father about this problem.
    You ought to tell your father about this problem.

●   Indicating a probable future event: **should** and **ought to** have similar
    meanings:
    They should be here soon.
    They ought to be here soon.

●   In reported speech, **should** is used instead of **shall** (⇨ exercise 120):
    I asked if I should open the door.

●   **must** and **have to** have similar meanings in the positive, but **must** is
    sometimes used to show a position of authority:
    Parent to child: '*You must be back by seven o'clock.*'
    (here, the authority comes from the speaker)
    One friend to another: '*You'll have to get up early to catch the morning
    train.*'
    (here, the obligation comes from the situation)

⇨ exercises 100 and 101 for past tenses.

Put **should**, **ought to**, **must** or **have to** in the sentences below, using
negatives or questions if necessary. Sometimes more than one answer is
possible, but you should write one only:

1   They .... be arriving in a few hours.
     They should / ought to be arriving in a few hours.
2   We .... to go home at twelve because my mother wants the car.
     We have to go home at twelve because my mother wants the car.
3   They insisted that we .... have a meal.
4   There are no trains today, so we .... to go by car.
5   I think you .... tell your parents you're going to be late. They'll be
     worried.

6 You . . . . never do that again!
7 The manager suggested that we . . . . try to find another hotel.
8 You . . . . see that film if you get the chance.
9 According to our information, the President . . . . be re-elected.
10 Do you think we . . . . ask before we borrow the car?
11 You . . . . come if you don't want to.
12 You . . . . be smoking at your age.
13 He asked me anxiously what he . . . . do next.
14 Do you think I . . . . tell the teacher what happened?
15 My boss told me that I . . . . be late.

95 ★★
may, might

● **may** and **might** indicate present or future possibility:
  He might arrive soon.
  He may arrive soon.
  She might be angry if you do that.
  She may be angry if you do that.

● **May I**? or **May we**? are used for polite requests, in the same way as
  Can I? or **Can we**? (⇨ exercise 89). It is a very polite form:
  May I ask you a question?
  May I have a glass of water, please?

NOTES

* **may** is occasionally used in formal English to mean **to be allowed to**:
  Guests may bring husbands or wives if they wish.

* **may** and **might** are usually used in question form only with **I** or **we**:
  other persons more often use the positive with **Do you think . . .?**:
  He might be late. → Do you think he might be late?

* The negative of **may** is **may not**. (NOT ~~mayn't~~).
  The negative of **might** is **might not** or **mightn't**.

* For **might have** and **may have** ⇨ exercises 100 and 101.

Rewrite these sentences using **may** or **might**. Where two answers are
possible, write them both:

1 Maybe he'll get a new job.
   He might get a new job. / He may get a new job.
2 Do you think I could have one of these cakes?
   May I have one of these cakes?
3 Maybe there's some tea in the pot.
4 Would you mind if I asked you how old you are?
5 Visitors are not allowed to stay in the hospital after ten p.m.
6 Do you think I could have one of these sandwiches?
7 I think the car is in the station car park.
8 Is it alright if I use your phone?

9   Guests are allowed to wear casual dress.
10 Maybe she'll move to London.
11 There's a possibility that the show will be cancelled.
12 Maybe she'll be elected.
13 I think that Andrew will collect the money.
14 Maybe Peter won't come to the cinema tomorrow.
15 Maybe it'll rain this afternoon.

96 ★★
need + infinitive

- *Positive:*
  I need to practise my English.

- *Negative:*
  a) **don't need to** is generally used when the situation does not require
     something to be done:
     You don't need to have a visa to go to France from Britain.

  b) **needn't** is generally used when the speaker gives the authority for
     something not being done:
     Teacher to students: '*You needn't do any homework tonight.*'

- *Questions:*
  a) *Do I need to apply for a visa?*
  b) *Need I do any homework this weekend?*

* Note the use of **to** in the examples.

Write the correct form of **need** to complete these sentences:

1   The teacher says we . . . . go to school tomorrow. (negative)
    The teacher says we needn't go to school tomorrow.
2   . . . . I . . . . have a licence to drive a car in this country? (question)
    Do I need to have a licence to drive a car in this country?
3   I've told her that she . . . . to work harder. (positive)
4   You . . . . take any equipment – the school provides it. (negative)
5   . . . . I . . . . phone you before I come to see you? (question)
6   My mother says I . . . . do the washing-up today. (negative)
7   You . . . . have more experience before you apply for this job. (positive)
8   You can go home now, you . . . . stay any longer. (negative)
9   You . . . . work here to be able to use the tennis court. (negative)
10 You . . . . say any more: I agree with you. (negative)

97 ★★★
need as a main verb and need + gerund

- **need** can be used as a *main verb*:
  I need some petrol.
  Do you need anything else?

- **need** can be used with the *gerund*, with the same meaning as a passive construction:
  My car needs cleaning. (= My car needs to be cleaned)
  Your hair needs washing. (= Your hair needs to be washed)

Rewrite these sentences using the correct form of **need**. It will be necessary to change some words:

1   I think it's time for your house to be painted.
    Your house needs painting.
2   How many people should we have for a full team?
    How many people do we need for a full team?
3   It's important for this job that we should have more time.
4   This floor is dirty: it should be cleaned immediately.
5   The doctor says that I should have more exercise.
6   Your tyres are very old. It's time to change them.
7   How much food should we have for the weekend?
8   How much money should we have for the trip?
9   The dog's hungry. It wants to be fed.
10 The baby's dirty. It's time to wash her.

98   ★★★
need in the past

- *Positive:*
  I needed something to eat.
  I needed to rest for a few minutes.
  The house needed painting.

- *Negative:*
  a) **didn't need to** + *infinitive*
     I didn't need to get up early yesterday. (= it wasn't necessary, so I didn't)
  b) **needn't have** + *past participle*
     I needn't have got up early yesterday. (= it wasn't necessary, but I did it, and now I realize that it wasn't necessary)

Write **didn't need to** or **needn't have** and the correct form of the verb to complete these sentences:

1   I .... (catch) the bus this morning, because Vic gave me a lift.
    I didn't need to catch the bus this morning, because Vic gave me a lift.
2   I .... (lend) him that money. I found out later that he had already borrowed all the money he wanted.
    I needn't have lent him that money.
3   I .... (do) that homework – the teacher didn't even look at it.
4   I .... (take) a tent, because I knew I could hire one at the campsite.
5   You .... (buy) such an expensive present, but I'm very glad that you did.
6   I .... (take) any money: they had already told me that it wasn't necessary.

7   I . . . . (count) the money: they had already told me that it was done
    automatically.
8   I . . . . (work) so hard for my exams: they were much easier than I
    expected them to be.
9   I . . . . (get up) so early: I had forgotten it was Saturday.
10 I had some friends in the town, so I . . . . (stay) in a hotel.

99 ★★★
need: check

Put the verbs in the sentences below into the correct form, adding **to** where
necessary:

1   I (not need / fix) my bike yesterday – I could have used my father's.
    I needn't have fixed my bike yesterday – I could have used my father's.
2   I think the house (need / paint) now.
    I think the house needs painting now.
3   You're never here when I (need) you.
    You're never here when I need you.
4   You (not need / stay) any longer, boys – you can go home now.
5   How much money (I need) for the weekend?
6   I (not need / take) the car – we could have used Jenny's.
7   I know I (not need / get up) early yesterday – I forgot it was a Saturday.
8   The room's rather dirty, I'm afraid – it (need / clean).
9   I stopped at the hotel because I (need / have) a rest.
10 You (not need / send) it by post – I could have picked it up.
11 Pat's a clever student, but she (need / work) harder.
12 The prisoners were told that they (not need / do) any more work.
13 There were no customs officers, so we (not need / show) our
    passports.
14 (You need / have) a special licence to drive a lorry?
15 You (not need / worry) Peter, everything will be alright.

100 ★★★
Modals in the past tense

FORM

modal + **have** + past participle			
I He She It We You They	should could may might would must ought to can't	have	known. arrived. gone.

- *Positive:*
  I should have known.
  He might have arrived.
  They ought to have gone.

- *Question:*
  Should I have known?
  Ought they to have gone?
  Could he have arrived?

- *Negative:*
  I shouldn't have gone.
  He couldn't have arrived.
  They oughtn't to have gone.

* Note that **have** stays the same for all persons (**he**, **she**, etc), as this is
  the perfect infinitive (⇨ exercise 114).

Put these sentences into the past, using the *perfect infinitive*:

1   You shouldn't say that.
     You shouldn't have said that.
2   They might not go.
     They might not have gone.
3   She couldn't know.
4   The machine ought to work.
5   They can't leave.
6   We ought to stop them.
7   Should I tell the teacher?
8   Could they help me?
9   Ought I to stay?
10   He can't be there.
11   They might not like it.
12   He may agree.
13   Shouldn't he say something?
14   Couldn't John drive the car?
15   Shouldn't he check the information?

101 ★★★
Modals in the past tense: different meanings

- **should** and **ought to** have their normal meaning in the past:
  You shouldn't have done that.
  You ought to have warned me about him.

- **may** and **might** have their normal meaning in the past.
  John might have told Mrs Jones what happened.
  Sheila may have left two or three days ago.

- **could** and **must** in the past are used to indicate deduction. **must have** is more certain than **could have**:
  Mike could have stayed in this hotel. (= it is possible that he stayed in this hotel)
  Mike must have stayed in this hotel. (= it is almost definite that he stayed in this hotel)

- **can't have** and **couldn't have** indicate a negative deduction. They are used as the negative for **must have**:

  Mike can't have stayed in this hotel. (= it is almost definite that he didn't stay in this hotel)

- **could have** = it was possible, but I didn't do it:
  I could have left at ten o'clock, but I didn't.

NOTES

*   In the present, **must be**, **have to be**, **could be** and **can't be** can indicate deduction:
     He's late – something must be wrong!

⇨ exercise 92 for **had to**.
⇨ exercise 90 for **was able to**.
⇨ exercise 98 for **need** in the past.
⇨ exercise 82 for **could have**, **would have**,
     and **might have** in the conditional.

Put **could**, **must**, **should**, **might**, or **can't** in the past tense in the spaces provided. Sometimes more than one answer is possible, but you should write one only:

1   How did you know about the wedding? Someone . . . . (tell) you!
     How did you know about the wedding? Someone must have told you!
2   The money was on the desk: I . . . . (take) it, but I didn't.
     The money was on the desk: I could have taken it, but I didn't.
3   I know you were angry, but you . . . . (not be) so rude.
4   I don't know who sent these flowers: it . . . . (be) Jane.
5   She . . . . (not move) abroad – she hates foreign countries.
6   . . . . (you not be) just a little more polite?
7   They . . . . (not know) about the plans for the new factory – it's not possible.
8   I think you . . . . (tell) your parents you were going to be late. They were very worried.
9   They . . . . (not get) into the house through a window: they were all closed.

10   They . . . . (not leave) without being seen by anybody.
11   I . . . . (go) for a swim if I'd wanted to.
12   You . . . . (apologize) for being late.
13   We don't know who took the money. The office was full of people and it . . . . (be) any of them.
14   I . . . . (not say) such a terrible thing.
15   I . . . . (not leave) my keys at home – I'm sure they were in my pocket.
16   He . . . . (warn) us that he was going to leave his job.
17   She tried to contact me, but the phone . . . . (be) engaged.
18   He . . . . (not know) about her illness – nobody had told him about it.
19   I don't know who wrote the letter. It . . . . (not be) Mrs Johnson, as she wasn't in the office that day.
20   I'm sorry, I . . . . (let) you know what was happening.

102 ★★★
could, would, might

- ● *+ infinitive*
  could = ability or possibility in the present or future:
  I could do it if you wanted me to.
  would = conditional intention in the present or future:
  I would do it if I were able to.
  might = possibility in the present or future:
  I might do it.

- ● *+ perfect infinitive*
  could = ability or possibility in the past:
  He could have gone early, but he didn't.
  would = intention in the past:
  He would have gone early if they had let him.
  might = possibility in the past:
  He might have gone early – I don't know.

- ● *Indirect speech:*
  can ⟶ could: *We knew that he could be annoying.*
  will ⟶ would: *We knew that he would be annoying.*
  may/might → might: *We knew that he might be annoying.*

- ● *Requests:*
  Could }
  Would } *you open the door for me, please?*

- ● *Offers:*
  Could *I do it for you?*

Put **could**, **would**, or **might** in the correct form to complete these sentences. Give all the answers possible for each sentence:

1   I . . . . seen Janice at the party last night. What does she look like?
    I might / could have seen Janice at the party last night.
2   I'm sure I (not) . . . . done it if I hadn't been so angry.
    I'm sure I wouldn't have done it if I hadn't been so angry.

3   We thought that he . . . . be disappointed.
     We thought that he could / would / might be disappointed.
4   I . . . . give it to her tomorrow.
5   I . . . . be a bit more careful if I were you.
6   The train . . . . be an hour or two late.
7   You (not) . . . . been at the restaurant yesterday – I looked everywhere
     for you.
8   Put some food in your bag – the journey . . . . take hours.
9   She told me that the children . . . . be very noisy in the evening.
10   I thought that the shop . . . . be closed by seven o'clock.
11   . . . . you work if you weren't paid for it?
12   We didn't know what the noise was – it . . . . been anything.
13   I . . . . spoken to your boss if I'd seen her.
14   There . . . . be several reasons for the accident.
15   By half-past eight I knew that she (not) . . . . come.
16   . . . . you hold my coat for a minute?
17   Be careful when you go abroad – anything . . . . happen.
18   I . . . . said I was sorry, but I didn't.
19   They warned me that I . . . . not get the job.
20   . . . . I ask you a few questions?

Gerunds and infinitives

The gerund

103 ⋆
The gerund

●   The *gerund* is used like a noun:
    Smoking is bad for you.
    Do you like **watching** TV?
    She's good at **swimming**.

●   It is formed by adding **ing** to the infinitive:
    go ⟶ go**ing**
    stay ⟶ stay**ing**
    The negative is formed by adding **not**:
    Would you mind **not smoking**?

⋆   Note the changes that are sometimes necessary:
    li**e** ⟶ l**y**ing (**ie → y**)
    tak**e** → tak**ing** (vowel + consonant + **e**: **e** is omitted)
    sit ⟶ sit**ting** (single vowel + single consonant → single
    vowel + double consonant)

103a Write the gerund of these verbs:

do	swim	fly
play	run	try
travel	lie	get
ride		

103b Fill the gaps with gerunds from the above list. Use each verb once only:

1   She likes . . . . every morning before breakfast.
    She likes running every morning before breakfast.
2   After . . . . my homework, I usually watch TV.
3   I enjoy . . . . on the beach.
4   She doesn't like . . . . with other children.
5   . . . . is a fast way of . . . . .
6   She likes sport, especially . . . . horses and . . . . .
7   After . . . . several times, I finally passed my exams.
8   I lay in bed and thought about . . . . up.

104 ☒
like, dislike and other verbs + gerund

- Some verbs are usually followed by a gerund or a noun, including the following:

like	love	finish	start
dislike	hate	stop	enjoy
prefer	miss	give up	begin

*   Note that **like**, **love**, **prefer**, and **start** are sometimes followed by the infinitive ⇨ exercise 115.

⇨ exercise 70 for verbs followed by the gerund, infinitive, or indirect speech.

Write these sentences changing the verbs into gerunds:

1   Do you like (smoke)?
    Do you like smoking?
2   I dislike (get up) at seven o'clock every morning.
3   I started (work) here eight or nine years ago.
4   Do you prefer (travel) by plane or by ship?
5   I hate (write) 'thank you' letters.
6   I gave up (drive) after I had a bad accident.
7   I miss (be) able to visit my family.
8   I love (sit) here by the sea in the evenings.
9   I think it's time to stop (play) football.
10 What time did you finish (read) last night?
11 Why don't you like (go) to discos?
12 I think I'll start (pack) my suitcase.
13 I enjoy (play) tennis, but I don't like (watch) it.
14 What time will you finish (study) today?
15 I can't understand people who don't like (dance).

105 ☒☒
Prepositions + gerund

- When a verb follows a preposition, it takes the gerund:
    We thought **about leaving** early.
    I was worried **about getting** home.
    I'm interested **in hearing** more about your offer.
    I'm tired **of hearing** his excuses.
    After closing the door, he looked up and down the street.
    Check your passport **before leaving**.

NOTES

*   Note that **to** can be a preposition, or part of an infinitive:
    I decided to leave early. (**to** + infinitive)
    I'm looking forward to seeing them again. (**to** + gerund)

*   A gerund behaves like a noun. Where a gerund can be used, a noun
      can also be used:
      I'm looking forward to going on holiday.
      I'm looking forward to my holiday.

Complete these sentences putting the verbs into the gerund, using a
preposition from this list:

about	of	in	to	after
about	of	in	to	by
about	for	on	at	without

1   We talked . . . . (go) to France for our holiday.
     We talked about going to France for our holiday.
2   I look forward . . . . (see) you again next year.
3   She's tired . . . . (work) for the company.
4   I'm very happy . . . . my parents (come) home.
5   . . . . (open) the front door, I walked slowly through it.
6   We got into the house . . . . (climb) through a window.
7   I'm looking forward . . . . (work) with you.
8   Are you interested . . . . (join) the committee?
9   I'm tired . . . . (come) to the same place every week.
10   He's very keen . . . . (swim) at the moment.
11   I'm worried . . . . Jayne (get) to the airport on time.
12   I'm not interested . . . . (hear) your excuses.
13   She's very good . . . . (listen) to what people say.
14   This is used . . . . (cut) metal.
15   The car drove off . . . . (stop).

106 ★★★
Person + gerund

●   In formal English *possessive + gerund* can be used:
     *I have no objection to **your arriving** late.*
     *We are concerned about **the company's trading** in oil.*

●   In conversational English, the possessive is not used: the *object* form
     is used instead:
     *I don't mind **him coming** late.*
     *We are worried about **Jane working** so hard.*

Supply both the possessive and object form of the words provided:

1   I don't like . . . . asking him to stay. (you)
     I don't like your asking him to stay.
     I don't like you asking him to stay.
2   Do you mind . . . . smoking? (I)
3   They tried to stop . . . . singing. (we)

4   They don't understand . . . . leaving home when he did. (John)
5   I'm worried about . . . . taking so much money. (she)
6   I didn't like . . . . lending the car to him. (you)
7   What do you think about . . . . resigning? (Tom)
8   I'm bored with . . . . complaining. (they)
9   Do you know the reason for . . . . stopping work? (they)
10   Who told you about . . . . being sacked? (he)
11   What do you think of . . . . leaving the country like that? (they)
12   I can think of no reason for . . . . saying that. (she)
13   I don't like . . . . being out so late. (he)
14   She's worried about . . . . being arrested. (we)
15   The firm doesn't mind . . . . arriving at ten o'clock. (I)

107 ★★
Gerunds as subjects of sentences

●   Gerunds can be *subjects* of sentences (or *objects* ➪ exercise 103):
       Smoking *makes me feel sick.*
       Living *in a foreign country can be very difficult.*

Rewrite these sentences starting with a gerund. You may need to change some words:

1   A good way of keeping fit is to swim every day.
     Swimming every day is a good way of keeping fit.
2   It takes a long time to learn a foreign language.
3   Clean the machine more often – that will solve your problems.
4   Grow your own food. It's less expensive.
5   Give up smoking: it will make you feel better.
6   It is cheaper to go by rail than by air.
7   You are not allowed to smoke here.
8   It's not very pleasant to be in hospital.
9   It's very difficult to windsurf properly.
10   It's more difficult to speak a foreign language than to read it.
11   It is forbidden to walk on the grass.
12   One thing I can't do is swim on my back.
13   It's difficult to be polite to someone you don't like.
14   It's not easy to change money here on a Saturday.
15   It is impossible to park your car during office hours.

108 ★★
Gerunds: check

have	study	smoke	work	live
move	get up	say	go	make
watch	help	eat	write	see
learn	look after	become	walk	go out

Write the verbs in the box in the correct form in these sentences.
Use each verb once only.

1   . . . . is unhealthy, but a lot of people find it difficult to stop.
     Smoking is unhealthy, but a lot of people find it difficult to stop.
2   I'm fed up with . . . . in the city – it's too dirty and crowded.
3   I enjoy . . . . in the garden at weekends.
4   I have decided to stop . . . . in the evenings so that I can save some
     money for my holidays.
5   He's an artistic person – very good at . . . . poetry.
6   They don't like . . . ., and go everywhere by car.
7   I'm not really interested in . . . . to university.
8   She's going to continue . . . . for another two years, until her exams.
9   They're thinking of . . . . house.
10   That machine? Oh, it's used for . . . . toasted sandwiches.
11   They've given up . . . . meat.
12   Before . . . . a teacher, he worked in advertising.
13   . . . . children can be very tiring.
14   We're looking forward to . . . . you.
15   They hate . . . . early in the morning.
16   Thank you for . . . . me organize the party.
17   They're very keen on . . . . how to play chess.
18   We love . . . . parties.
19   She left without . . . . goodbye.
20   . . . . television seems to be our national sport.

The infinitive

FORM

● Depending on the construction, infinitives are used with or without **to**:

   *It's time **to go**.*
   *Did you see the accident **happen**?*

109 ⊠
to + infinitive after certain verbs

● Certain verbs take the *infinitive* (⇨ exercise 70 for a list).

   I want to stay.
   We decided to wait for the bus.

*   Note the *negative*:

   We decided not to wait for the bus.

Complete the sentences, using a verb from the box.
Use each verb once only:

help	stay	find
speak	look after	telephone
buy	go	go out
get on		

1 We decided . . . . to Spain for our holidays.
   We decided to go to Spain for our holidays.
2 She learnt . . . . Arabic when she was a child.
3 I tried . . . . you but there was no answer.
4 They refused . . . . the plane.
5 She hopes . . . . a job soon.
6 Did you forget . . . . the bread?
7 I'm tired: I don't want . . . . tonight.
8 They offered . . . . the children for the evening.
9 They're planning . . . . with us for the weekend.
10 He agreed . . . . us with our problem.

110 ★★
to + infinitive to express purpose

● **to** + *infinitive* is used to express purpose:

   *I came here **to see** you.*
   *I went to London **to study** English.*
   *I drove to the airport **to meet** my parents.*

Express each question and answer as one sentence, using **to** + *infinitive*.
Note that you will need to change some words:

1 Q: Why do you go to the beach every weekend?
   A: Because I like swimming.
   She . . . .
   She goes to the beach every weekend to swim.
2 Q: Why did you move to London?
   A: I wanted to find work.
   He . . . .
3 Q: Why are you leaving home?
   A: I'm going to university in Birmingham.
   She . . . .
4 Q: Why are you having a party?
   A: It's my thirtieth birthday, and I want to celebrate it.
   He . . . .
5 Q: Why do you get up at six every morning?
   A: I do my training then.
   She . . . .

6   Q: Why are you going out?

     A: I want to telephone my mother.

     He . . . .

7   Q: Why are you saving money?

     A: We want to buy a car.

     They . . . .

8   Q: Why are you going to Egypt?

     A: We want to visit Ali's parents.

     They . . . .

9   Q: Why did you buy a new suit?

     A: I want to wear it at the office party.

     He . . . .

10   Q: Why did you hire a video?

     A: We want to record the World Cup Final.

     They . . . .

111 ★★
to + infinitive after nouns and adjectives

to + *infinitive* can be used

●   after certain adjectives:

     I was pleased to see them again.

     I'm surprised to hear you say that.

     Note the expression **too . . . to**:

     It was too hot to go out.

●   after certain nouns and pronouns, to show what is to be done with them or how they are to be used:

     I've got some homework to do.

     Is there anyone else to see?

     Note the expression **enough . . . to**:

     Have we got enough money to go to the cinema?

Put these sentences in the correct order, making one verb an *infinitive*, and writing the other in the *present simple*:

1   Plane catch she a have.

     She has a plane to catch.

2   Lot of a housework there be do.

     There is a lot of housework to do.

3   Who something eat want?

4   Smoke he young be too.

5   Come expect Jane I.

6   Delighted hear I be the news.

7   Have books some I read.

8   Illness surprised hear I be his of.

9   Nothing children the have do.

10   Letters I write some have.

11   Shopping some he do have.

12   Nothing say have I.
13   Always much eat have you too to.
14   Outside cold eat it too be.
15   Lovely see it again you be.

112 ★★★
it + to + infinitive

to + *infinitive* is used

●   after **that / it / there** + **to be** + *adjective* + *noun*:

> *That was a stupid thing **to do**.*
> *It was a strange thing **to say**.*
> *There are other people **to see**.*

●   after **it** + **to be** + *adjective*. This sometimes uses **of you**, **of him**, etc:

> *It was nice **of you to come**.*
> *It was kind **of them to send** me money.*
> *It was good **to see** them again.*
> *It was difficult **to drive** the car with one hand.*

Rewrite these sentences, starting with the words given. You will need to change some words:

1   Why did he ask that question? It was very strange.
     That . . . .
     That was a very strange question to ask.
2   Thank you for visiting Janice in hospital. It was very kind.
     It . . . .
     It was very kind of you to visit Janice in hospital.
3   Why did he make that remark? It was very rude.
     That . . . .
4   I enjoyed flying in the plane. It was very exciting.
     It . . . .
5   I'm pleased I saw her again. It was quite a surprise.
     It . . . .
6   John gave them £100. It was very generous.
     It . . . .
7   I couldn't drive the car. It was very difficult.
     It . . . .
8   Why did you visit that place? It was very odd.
     That . . . .
9   Why did he do that? It was very silly.
     It . . . .
10   He shouldn't have driven the car like that. It was stupid.
     It . . . .

113 ★★
Use of the infinitive without **to**

The *infinitive without* **to** is used:

● after **will**, **can**, **must**, etc (⇨ exercise 88)

● after **make** and **let** + noun/pronoun:
*He made me **do** it.*
*We let them **go** home.*

● after verbs of **seeing**, **hearing**, and **feeling** + noun/pronoun:
*I saw him **arrive**.*
*We watched them **go**.*
*I felt him **move**.*

★ Note that verbs of **seeing**, **hearing** or **feeling** can also use the
present participle:
*I saw him **arrive**.*
*I saw him **arriving**.*

Rewrite the sentences, using the words given. You may need to change
some words:

1   He arrived early. (I saw)
     I saw him arrive early.
2   I didn't want to stay at home. (They made me)
     They made me stay at home.
3   She got out of the car. (We watched)
4   They allowed me to telephone my lawyer. (They let)
5   They left at eleven o'clock. (I heard)
6   The policeman told me to empty my pockets. (The policeman made)
7   The dog jumped through the window. (I saw)
8   Maybe the school will ask me to pay extra. (Do you think the school
     will make)
9   The animal moved. I felt it. (I felt the)
10   I want to leave the country. (Do you think the government will let)

114 ★★★
The perfect infinitive

FORM

● The *perfect infinitive* is formed with **have** + *past participle*:

    go→ *have gone* or *to have gone*

    see→ *have seen* or *to have seen*

USE

● in the *third conditional* (⇨ exercise 82) with **would**, **might**, or **could**:
    If he'd phoned, I would have met him at the airport.

- with **could**, **must**, **need**, **can't**, **might**, etc in the past (⇨ exercise 100)
  Who could have told him the news?

- after verbs such as **want**, **expect**, and **hope** as a *future perfect*. This
  form uses **to**:
  I hope to have finished this by Christmas.

- after certain adjectives, as a past. This form uses **to**:
  I was disappointed to have missed him.

Put the verbs in brackets into the *perfect infinitive*. Use **to** where necessary:

1   I expect (finish) working here by the end of the year.
     I expect to have finished working here by the end of the year.
2   They can't (know) what was going to happen.
     They can't have known what was going to happen.
3   The children are very pleased (finally meet) their uncle.
4   We hope (contact) all the record manufacturers in Britain when we
     finish the survey.
5   I expect (collect) £3,000 by this time next year.
6   If I'd known he was in hospital, I would (visit) him.
7   I was disappointed (miss) such a good opportunity.
8   I want (finish) the job by the time I go home.
9   We were very pleased (be able to) help.
10   Lots of people could (tell) the newspapers what happened.

115 ★★★
Gerund or infinitive?

CONTRAST

- Some verbs use only the gerund, and some verbs use only the
  infinitive. Certain verbs use the gerund *and* the infinitive
  (⇨ exercise 70 for a full list).

- The gerund is used:
  a) after prepositions (⇨ exercise 105).
  b) as verbal nouns (⇨ exercises 104 and 107).
  c) after certain idioms such as **can't stand**, **can't bear**, etc.

- The infinitive is used:
  a) after certain nouns or adjectives (⇨ exercise 111).
  b) to express purpose (⇨ exercise 110).
  c) after **it** + **to be** + *adjective / noun* (⇨ exercise 112).

- Some verbs (e.g. **love**, **hate**, **start**, **prefer**) can take gerund or
  infinitive, with similar meanings:
  I love to visit old houses.
  I love visiting old houses.
  I started to polish the car, but then decided not to.
  I started polishing the car, but then decided not to.

● **remember**, **stop**, and **try** have a different meaning with the gerund or the infinitive:
   a) *I remembered to give him the money.*
      (= the remembering happened *before* the giving)
      I remembered giving him the money.
      (= the remembering happened *after* the giving)
   b) *I stopped to watch the carnival.*
      (= I stopped because I wanted to watch the carnival)
      I stopped watching the carnival.
      (= I had been watching the carnival: then I stopped watching)
   c) *I tried to open the door, but it was locked.*
      (= I didn't open it)
      I tried opening the door to let in some fresh air.
      (= I did open it)

Put the verb in the *gerund* or the *infinitive*:

1   . . . . is really good fun. (fly)
    Flying is really good fun.
2   We stopped at the motorway services . . . . something . . . . (get / eat)
    We stopped at the motorway services to get something to eat.
3   'What's this for?'
    'It's for . . . . vegetables.' (cook)
4   I can't get used to . . . . before the dawn. (get up)
5   I'm sorry about . . . . you. (not invite)
6   There's a lot of work . . . . on the new building. (do)
7   I really love . . . . with the children. (play)
8   . . . . is a good form of exercise. (swim)
9   There are some very interesting things . . . . in the British Museum. (see)
10 You're lucky you haven't got a child . . . . . (look after)
11 We managed . . . . the exam by . . . . each other's answers. (pass / copy)
12 Dave decided . . . . Sheila for a week or two. (not phone)
13 I can't stand . . . . the washing-up. (do)
14 I think I'm going to have to give up . . . . football. (play)
15 It really is time . . . . . (go)
16 I've decided . . . . here for another year. (not stay)
17 I know the keys are here: I remember . . . . somewhere. (put them down)
18 We were getting tired, so we stopped . . . . lunch. (have)
19 I tried . . . . some salt, but it didn't help. (add)
20 I'm looking forward to . . . . the programme. (see)
21 I went home . . . . that the children were alright. (check)
22 You're much too young . . . . in there. (go)
23 I was surprised . . . . about the new baby. (not hear)
24 We're very keen on . . . . the team. (join)
25 It was a very odd thing . . . . . (say)
26 We decided . . . . until the end of the film. (not stay)

27 I miss . . . . to see my parents every day. (be able)
28 They wouldn't let me . . . . in the driving-seat. (sit)
29 It's your last chance . . . . you're sorry. (say)
30 We agreed . . . . any more work. (not do)

Reported speech

There are two ways of reporting what a person says:

- *Direct speech*
  He said, 'I'm going home.'
  'I'm going home,' he said.

- *Indirect speech*
  He says he's going home.
  He said he was going home.

Direct speech

116 ⋆
Writing direct speech

She said, 'My name's Stella.'
'My name's Stella,' she said.

- Direct speech reports the exact words the speaker says. Put quotation marks ('. . . .') before and after the speaker's statement.

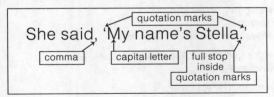

She said, 'My name's Stella.'
comma · quotation marks · capital letter · full stop inside quotation marks

NOTES

⋆ the speaker's statement always starts with a capital letter.

⋆ **she said** can go before or after the statement, but is separated from it by a comma (,). Commas and full stops after the statement go inside the quotation marks.
  'How are you?' she said.

Put the sentences below into *direct speech* using the words given.

1 the bus driver
The bus driver said,
'We're late.'

2 the little boy

3 Jane

4 the policeman

5 the old man

6 the teacher

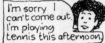

7 she

8 he

9 the guard

10 the receptionist

---

117 ★★
say, tell

CONTRAST

● **tell** has a *personal direct object* (e.g. **me**, **him**, **her**, etc ➪
   exercise 131)

   She told me she was going to be late.
   'It's too late,' she told me.
   (We cannot say: ~~He told the weather was nice.~~)

● **tell** is not used before questions. (We cannot say: ~~He told~~
   ~~me, 'Have we met before?'~~)

● **say** never has a *personal direct object*:

   She said she was going to be late.
   'It's too late,' she said.

   The *indirect object* (**to me**, **to her**, **to us**, etc ➪ exercise 131) is used
   instead:

   'I don't like them very much,' she said to me quietly.
   Why did he say that to you?

*   There are a few special phrases in which **tell** does not have to take a personal direct object:

> tell the truth   tell the time
> tell a lie   tell a story
> tell lies

Use the correct form of **say** or **tell** in these sentences:

1   She . . . . me she didn't agree.
     She told me she didn't agree.
2   He . . . ., 'Have we met before?'
     He said, 'Have we met before?'
3   I . . . . them I wasn't happy with their work.
4   She . . . . me a story about her parents.
5   He . . . ., 'Are you feeling OK?'
6   She smiled, and . . . . to me, 'I'm very pleased to meet you.'
7   I didn't hear: what did she . . . .?
8   Could you . . . . me the time please?
9   They . . . . me they were going to a meeting.
10   I . . . . the policeman my address.
11   I . . . . I wanted to buy a magazine.
12   He . . . . he wasn't interested in politics.
13   Could you . . . . me your name again please?
14   Do you think he's . . . . the truth?
15   Would you . . . . them to come early tomorrow?
16   If he . . . . that again there'll be trouble.
17   I . . . . them it was dangerous to swim here.
18   Did you . . . . anything to him about your problems at work?
19   . . . . me what happened.
20   I think he's . . . . lies.

Indirect speech

118 ★★
Reported statements with no change of tense

●   When the main verb of the sentence is *present*, *present perfect*, or *future* there is no change of tense in the reported statement:

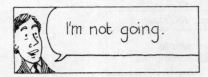

I'm not going.

= He says **he isn't** going.

= He'll say **he isn't** going.

= He's said **he isn't** going.

*   **that** can be used after the main verb. The use of **that** is optional:
*He says **that** he isn't going.*
He says he isn't going.

Write these sentences in *indirect speech*, using the words given. Remember to change the pronouns where necessary.

1   'I haven't done my homework.' (she says)
    She says she hasn't done her homework.
2   'I haven't got any money.' (he'll tell you)
    He'll tell you he hasn't got any money.
3   'I've seen the film before.' (she says)
4   'I want to go home.' (he's already told you)
5   'I haven't seen my mother for years.' (he says)
6   'I don't know how much it costs.' (she says)
7   'I don't like going to parties.' (she's told me)
8   'We've never been to Berlin.' (they say)
9   'I need the money to visit my parents.' (he'll say)
10   'We can't come on Tuesday.' (they've told me)
11   'I'm going to visit Europe this year.' (the president will announce that)
12   'I can't stand classical music.' (Mary tells me)
13   'The plane will land in half an hour.' (the pilot has just announced that)
14   'There are no tickets left for tonight's performance.' (the booking office says that)
15   'We haven't had anything to eat.' (the children say)
16   'I've already seen the play.' (he's told me)
17   'I'll come again next year.' (I've told them)
18   'I'm not feeling very well.' (Simon says)

119 ☒
Reported statements with a change of tense

●   When the *main verb* of the sentence is in the *past tense*, the tense in the reported statement is changed:

I'm not going.   = *He said **he wasn't** going.* or
    *He said that **he wasn't** going.*

My name's Stella.   = *She said her name **was** Stella.* or
    *She said that her name **was** Stella.*

FORM

Speaker's words	Reported statement
present simple ⟶	past simple
present continuous ⟶	past continuous

⟱ exercise 120 for other tense changes.

Write these sentences in *indirect speech*, using the words given. Change the pronouns where necessary:

1 'My name's Ian.' (he said)
   He said his name was Ian.
2 'I'm writing a letter.' (she said)
   She said she was writing a letter.
3 'I'm waiting for Joan.' (she said)
4 'I don't like the idea.' (he said)
5 'The car isn't at my house.' (she said)
6 'The washing machine's broken.' (he said)
7 'I'm working.' (he said)
8 'We're worried about Peter.' (they said)
9 'I don't smoke.' (Mary said)
10 'I'm waiting for my exam results.' (John said)
11 'I work for an American company.' (Mrs Johnson said)
12 'I feel ill.' (the little boy said)
13 'I'm watching television.' (Susan said)
14 'I like the new house.' (Mary said)
15 'I'm washing the car.' (Susan said)

120 ★★

Reported statements: tense changes

● When the *main verb* of the sentence is in the *past tense*, the tense in the reported statement is changed (⟱ exercise 119).

   'I'll talk to Mr Jones.' ⟶ He said he'd talk to Mr Jones.
   'I haven't seen anybody.' ⟶ She said she hadn't seen anybody.
   'I must go.' ⟶ He said he had to go.

● Tense changes when the main verb is past tense:

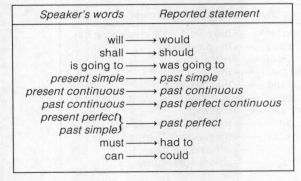

Speaker's words	Reported statement
will ⟶	would
shall ⟶	should
is going to ⟶	was going to
present simple ⟶	*past simple*
present continuous ⟶	*past continuous*
past continuous ⟶	*past perfect continuous*
present perfect⎫ ⟶ *past simple*⎭	*past perfect*
must ⟶	had to
can ⟶	could

- **that** is optional after the main verb:
  He said **that** he wasn't going.
  He said he wasn't going.

Write these sentences in *indirect speech*:

1   'I'm very tired,' she said.
     She said she was very tired.
2   'I'll see them soon,' he said.
     He said he would see them soon.
3   'I'm going to the cinema,' she said.
4   'I see the children quite often,' he said.
5   'I'm having a bath,' she said.
6   'I've already met their parents,' he said.
7   'I stayed in a hotel for a few weeks,' she said.
8   'I must go home to make the dinner,' he said.
9   'I haven't been waiting long,' she said.
10   'I'm listening to the radio,' he said.
11   'I'll tell them the news on Saturday,' she said.
12   'I like swimming, dancing, and playing tennis,' he said.
13   'I can drive,' she said.
14   'I walked home after the party,' he said
15   'I'm going to be sick,' she said.
16   'I must go out to post a letter,' he said.
17   'I spoke to Jane last week,' she said.
18   'I'm trying to listen to the music,' he said.
19   'I'll phone the office from the airport,' she said.
20   'I can't speak any foreign languages,' he said.

121 ★★
Reported statements: other changes

- As well as tense changes (⇨ exercise 120), other words in *direct speech* need to be changed when they are reported. Here are some examples:

Speaker's words	Reported statement
tomorrow ⟶	the next day / the following day
yesterday ⟶	the day before
here ⟶	there
this / that ⟶	the
this morning ⟶	that morning
today ⟶	that day
tonight ⟶	that night
next / on Tuesday ⟶	the following Tuesday
last Tuesday ⟶	the previous Tuesday
the day after tomorrow ⟶	in two days' time
ago ⟶	before / previously

* Note that these changes generally occur, but they are not automatic. They depend on when and where the statement is reported.

* Some verbs do not change:
  would ⟶ *would*, *could* ⟶ *could*, *might* ⟶ *might*, *should* ⟶ *should*, *ought to* ⟶ *ought to*

Write these sentences in *indirect speech*, changing words where necessary:

1 'I'll see you tomorrow,' she said.
  She said she'd see me the next day.
2 'I saw her today,' he said.
  He said he'd seen her that day.
3 'I don't like this film,' she said.
4 She said, 'We went swimming today.'
5 'I'll see Mary on Sunday,' she said.
6 'I met her about three months ago,' he said.
7 'Pete and Sue are getting married tomorrow,' she said.
8 'Stephen's bringing some records to the party tonight,' he said.
9 'I really like this furniture,' she said.
10 'My parents are arriving tomorrow,' she said.
11 'We visited her this morning,' they said.
12 'We'll see her next summer,' they said.
13 'They were here three months ago,' he said.
14 'I'm meeting them at four o'clock today,' he said.
15 'I can see you tomorrow,' she said.

122 ★★
Reported questions: **Wh** questions

● Most reported questions have a main verb in the past tense. They use the same tense changes and word changes as in *reported statements* (⇨ exercises 120 and 121).

● Reported questions change the word order of the original question:

  'What's the time?'
  She asked what time it was.
  (NOT ~~She asked what was the time.~~)

  'How's your mother?'
  He asked me how my mother was.
  (NOT ~~He asked me how was my mother.~~)

⇨ exercise 138 for a list of **wh** words.

* **ask** can be used in reported speech with or without a personal direct object:

  She asked me how I was.
  She asked how I was.

Write these sentences as reported questions using the words given.
Change **you** to **I**, etc where necessary:

1   'What's your name?' he asked. (wanted to know)
     He wanted to know what my name was.
2   'How old are you?' she said. (asked)
     She asked how old I was.
3   'When does the train leave?' I asked. (asked)
4   'How are you?' he said. (asked)
5   'Who did you see at the meeting?' my mother said. (wanted to know)
6   'Why did you take my wallet?' he asked. (wanted to know)
7   'How did you get to school?' she said. (asked)
8   'Where do you live?' the boy asked. (wanted to know)
9   'Why wasn't Judy at the party?' she asked. (asked)
10   'Why didn't you telephone?' my father asked. (wanted to know)
11   'Why are you so late?' the teacher asked. (demanded to know)
12   'Why didn't the police report the crime?' the judge asked. (inquired)
13   'Why won't you let me in?' he shouted. (demanded to know)
14   'What time does the plane arrive?' we asked. (inquired)
15   'Who do you want to talk to?' she said. (asked)

123 ★★
Reported questions: **if / whether**

● **If** or **whether** (the choice is optional) is used for reported questions
   that do not start with **wh** words (⇨ exercise 122).
   *He asked **if** I was hungry.*
   Note the word order change:
   *'**Are you** angry?'* ⟶ *He asked if **I was** angry.*
   *'**Did you see** the film?'* ⟶ *She asked whether **I had seen** the film.*

● Tense changes and other word changes are as shown in
   exercises 120 and 121.

Write these sentences as reported questions. Change **you** to **I**, etc where
necessary:

1   'Do you like Marlon Brando?', she asked.
     She asked if I liked Marlon Brando.
2   'Are you enjoying yourself?', he asked.
     He asked whether I was enjoying myself.
3   'Does your father work here?', she asked.
4   'Do you live near your family?', he asked.
5   'Are you a foreigner?', she asked.
6   'Have you met Danny before?', he asked.
7   'Are you hungry?', she asked.
8   'Did you borrow my dictionary?', he asked.
9   'Have you finished your exams?', she asked.
10   'Did you invite Judy and Pat?', he asked.
11   'Does your brother live in London?' she asked.
12   'Do you know who broke the window?', he asked.

13 'Did they tell you when they were leaving?', she asked.
14 'Did you lend them your camera?', he asked.
15 'Have you hurt yourself?', she asked.

124 ⭐⭐
Reported questions: check

Write these sentences in *indirect speech*, using **wanted to know** and the words given. Change **you** to **I**, etc where necessary, as in the examples:

1 'Which book did you take?' (he)
He wanted to know which book I had taken.
2 'Are you wearing your overcoat?' (she)
She wanted to know if / whether I was wearing my overcoat.
3 'Did you telephone your mother?' (he)
4 'Is the box made of cardboard?' (she)
5 'How much did it cost?' (he)
6 'Are you seeing the director tomorrow?' (she)
7 'What are you doing?' (he)
8 'How far do I have to walk?' (she)
9 'Have you had anything to eat?' (he)
10 'Are you in a hurry?' (she)
11 'When does the performance start?' (he)
12 'How long does the journey take?' (she)
13 'Where did you stay in Paris?' (he)
14 'Have you had any letters?' (she)
15 'Do you like having holidays abroad?' (he)
16 'Did you see the accident?' (she)
17 'Which school did you go to?' (he)
18 'When did you start learning Spanish?' (she)
19 'Are you French?' (he)
20 'Have you ever been to Japan?' (she)

125 ⭐⭐
Reported commands

● Reported commands use a *personal direct object* and the *infinitive*:

He told the children to stop.

*He told **them to stop**.*

● The negative uses **not** before **to** + *infinitive*:
'Don't stop!' ⟶ He told them not to stop.
'Don't go!' ⟶ He told me not to go.

✱ A number of verbs can be used for reported commands; e.g. **tell**, **order**, **command**, **warn**, **instruct**, etc.

⇨ exercise 126 for reported requests.

Write these sentences in *indirect speech*, using the words given. Note that some words may have to be changed:

1   'Sit down Mary.' (he told)
     He told Mary to sit down.
2   'Don't go near the sea, children.' (the children's mother warned)
     The children's mother warned them not to go near the sea.
3   'Don't be late, Tim.' (Tim's father told)
4   'Be quiet, children.' (the librarian told)
5   'Don't shoot, men!' (the officer ordered)
6   'Have your tickets ready, please.' (the inspector told us)
7   'Don't use the telephone after eleven o'clock.' (the landlady told us)
8   'Leave your keys on the desk, please.' (the receptionist told us)
9   'Have your passports ready, please.' (the customs officer told us)
10   'Finish the job tonight, please.' (my boss told me)
11   'Run!' (the general ordered the soldiers)
12   'Open the door, please.' (my mother told me)
13   'Don't spend too much money on your holiday.' (my father told me)
14   'Hurry up.' (he told me)
15   'Don't be frightened.' (she told me)

126 ★★
Reported requests

● Reported requests (when you are asking someone to do something for you) have the same grammatical form as reported commands (⇨ exercise 125):

   'Would you open the ⸱ ⸱or, please?'
   ⟶ *She asked me to open the door.*
   'Could you lend me some money, please?'
   ⟶ *He asked me to lend him some money.*

● Reported requests usually use **ask** as the main verb. There is an important difference in meaning between:

   *He **told** me to give him some money.* and
   *He **asked** me to give him some money.*

★ Note the difference between a reported offer and a reported request:

   a) offer:
      'Would you like a cigarette?'
      ⟶ *He asked if I would like a cigarette.*

   b) request:
      'Would you pass me a cigarette?'
      ⟶ *He asked me to pass him a cigarette.*

Write these sentences in *indirect speech*. If two answers are possible, write them both.

1   'Would you pass my suitcase, please?', he asked.
    He asked me to pass his suitcase.
2   'Would you like some coffee?', she asked.
    She asked if I would like some coffee.
3   'Would you take the children to school for me?', he asked.
4   'Would you sit down, please?', she asked.
5   'Would you talk more quietly, please?', he asked.
6   'Would you like a lift into town?', she asked.
7   'Could you tell me how much a return ticket costs?', he asked.
8   'Would you turn on the radio, please?', she asked.
9   'Would you move your car, please?', he asked.
10 'Would you like to eat in the hotel or in a restaurant?', she asked.
11 'Would you pass my cup, please?', he asked.
12 'Would you check the oil for me, please?', she asked.
13 'Would you turn the car engine off, please?', he asked.
14 'Could you tell me the exchange rate for dollars and pounds?', she asked.
15 'Would you check the bill for me, please?', he asked.

127 ★★★
Indirect speech: check

Complete these sentences with the correct form of the verbs.

1   He said he .... already .... to the manager. (speak)
    He said he had already spoken to the manager.
2   She asked me .... my shoes. (take off)
    She asked me to take off my shoes.
3   He wanted to know where I .... for the last few years. (live)
    He wanted to know where I had been living for the last few years.
4   I warned her .... too near the cliff edge. (not go)
5   I asked her if Mrs Brownlow .... just ..... (leave)
6   I told them .... they were in the right part of the train. (check)
7   He told me he .... for several days. (not eat)
8   We agreed that I .... them a few days later. (see)
9   They asked me if I .... a cup of tea. (like)
10 He begged her .... him some money, but she refused. (give)
11 The police ordered the crowd ..... (stay back)
12 She wants to know if the manager .... tomorrow. (come back)
13 The expression on his face told me that I .... late. (be)
14 We decided that the computer .... switched off. (have to be)
15 We advised the company .... a new factory. (open)
16 I asked him whether Mr Steadman .... yet. (register)
17 He ordered his soldiers .... there. (stay)
18 Your parents want to know if you .... a good time here. (have)
19 They told me that the train .... at that very moment. (leave)
20 I wanted to know how much money I .... in my bank account. (have)

21   Mr Jones wants to know why you suddenly . . . . to resign last week. (decide)
22   The other people in the flat asked me . . . . . (not smoke)
23   The publishers have told me that they . . . . my book. (not going to accept)
24   Do you think I . . . . rude yesterday? (be)
25   They told me I . . . . very polite the previous evening. (not be)
26   He indicated that he . . . . by nodding his head. (agree)
27   They shouted that they . . . . cross the river and that they . . . . back to the car. (cannot / going to go)
28   They asked me . . . . anything but just . . . . quietly. (not say / listen)
29   She asked when the plane . . . . the night before and whether it . . . . direct from Brussels. (arrive / come)
30   He asked whether I . . . . to Dr Jones when I was in hospital. (talk)

128 ★★★
Verbs used in reporting

● It is not always necessary to report all the words a person says: some verbs are used to provide a summary instead:
    'Oh, dear,' she said, 'I'm terribly sorry I'm late.'
    ⟶ *She apologized for being late.*
    'I know a good restaurant. Why don't we go there?' he said.
    ⟶ *He suggested that we should go to a restaurant.*

*   The verbs are followed by the *infinitive*, *gerund*, or *indirect speech* (⇨ exercise 70).

Rewrite these sentences, choosing the correct verb from the box for each sentence and using it with the construction shown. In some cases the verb may replace part of the sentence. Use each verb once only:

Verbs that take the *infinitive*:
advise, invite, offer, promise, refuse, remind, warn

Verbs that take the *gerund*:
apologize for, insist on, suggest

Verbs followed by *indirect speech*:
agree, announce, boast, claim, concede

---

1   'We're going to get married in June,' she said.
    She announced that they were going to get married in June.
2   'Don't go near that dog,' she told him.
3   After the meal, he said, 'Please don't argue – I'm going to pay.'
4   'I'm sorry I didn't write,' she said.
5   'Would you like to come round for dinner on Friday evening?' he asked them.
6   'I think you should give up smoking,' the doctor said to her.
7   'Alright, yes, I was wrong and you were right,' he said.

8   'Yes, I'll write every week,' she said.
9   'Shall I carry that suitcase for you?' she said.
10   'How about going to the theatre on Saturday?' he said.
11   'The newspaper report's not true,' said the Prime Minister.
12   'Don't forget to post that letter,' she said to him.
13   'Yes, it was a difficult exam,' the teacher said.
14   'No, I won't give you a pay rise,' the manager told her.
15   'My parents have got three cars,' she said.

129 ★★★
Reporting conversations: summarizing

● When we report conversations, we do not normally report everything
  that was said: we select the important parts. This is part of a 'phone
  conversation between Anne and Sue:

ANNE: Are you doing anything at the weekend?
SUE: No, we're not.
ANNE: Well, would you like to come and stay with us for the weekend? I
      know you're all in need of a rest.
SUE: Oh, that would be lovely! Thank you very much.
ANNE: Not at all, it will be nice to see you again.
SUE: The only problem is, I haven't told you yet, but we bought a dog
      last week.
ANNE: A dog! How nice!
SUE: Yes . . . we can leave him with Paul's parents.
ANNE: No, no, bring him. I'd love to see him.
SUE: No, I couldn't possibly. He's rather young and playful, and he
      might start eating your furniture!
ANNE: That doesn't matter, really. You know I like dogs, so do bring
      him.
SUE: Are you sure?
ANNE: Yes, of course.
SUE: Oh well, in that case I will . . .

This is how Sue describes the conversation to her husband Paul:
    'Anne has invited us to stay with her for the weekend. She thought we
    needed a rest! I explained that we'd bought a dog and said that we
    could leave him with your parents, but she insisted that we should
    bring him.'

Below is a conversation between Jane and David. Jane later describes the
conversation to her husband Peter. Write what she said, starting with: *'Oh, I
saw David today. He . . .'*

There is a model answer to this question in the key, but there are several
ways of summarizing the conversation.

JANE: My parents are coming this weekend. I don't know what we're
       going to do with them.

DAVID: Why don't you take them to that new French restaurant in town, 'Le Pain'? It really is good, honestly. Jackie and I went there last week and the food was fantastic. I'm sure your parents would like it.

JANE: Mm, that's a good idea. Do you think they'd let children in there?

DAVID: Oh, I think so. But why don't you leave the kids with us? Jackie and I would be happy to look after them. We're not going anywhere on Saturday night.

JANE: Well, that's very nice of you. Are you really sure that would be OK?

DAVID: Of course I'm sure.

JANE: Well, that's marvellous! We'll bring them round to you at about 7.30. I hope they won't give you any trouble . . .

DAVID: Of course they won't. They can watch the new video.

JANE: Have you got a new video? Jackie didn't say anything about that . . .

DAVID: Do you remember she was applying for a job with the BBC? Well, she got it – and the video comes with the job.

JANE: She got the job? That's great news!

DAVID: It's supposed to be a secret but everyone will know soon enough.

JANE: Well look, why don't you come round on Sunday for lunch and tell us all about it? My parents will be there but I know they'd love to see you again.

DAVID: OK, that's a lovely idea. We'll come round on Sunday . . .

Sentence structure

Word order

130 ☒
Subject, verb, object

- Every sentence has a *verb* (**go**, **stay**, **live**, **talk**, etc). The verb can be one word:

  He | ^vgoes.   She | ^vstays.   (*present simple*)

  or a group of words:

  They | ^vwere singing.   He | ^vwas laughing.   (*past continuous*)

- Nearly all sentences have a *subject* – the person or thing that 'does' the verb:

  ^sShe | understands.   ^sThey|'re working.   ^sThe baby|'s sleeping.

- Generally, there are two types of verb:

  a) verbs that take an object:

  She | hit | ^ohim.   I | like | ^othem.   They | took | ^othe money.

  b) verbs that do not take an object:

  I|'m talking.   We|'re waiting.   She|'s sleeping.

NOTES

* Some verbs can be type a) *or* type b):

  a) *She opened the door.*   b) *The door opened.*
  a) *I'm writing a letter.*   b) *I'm writing.*

Copy these sentences into your notebook, and label them *S*, *V*, and *O*:

1   ^sThe men | ^vare working.
2   ^sHe|'s going to write | ^oa letter.
3   ^sI| ^vdon't understand.
4   He didn't say anything.

5   I like ice cream.
6   They left.
7   We ate breakfast.
8   I didn't take your car.
9   They're waiting.
10   She's reading a book.
11   I'm going to visit my mother.
12   She isn't going to stay.
13   We were watching television.
14   I didn't see anything.
15   I don't agree.

131 ★★
Direct object and indirect object

● In simple sentences the *object* is easy to see:
  *She hit **him**.*
  *They took **the money**.*

● Some verbs, however, have two objects:
  *She gave **me the book**.* (= she gave the book to me)
  the book is the real object of this sentence. It tells us *what* she gave.
  This is the *direct object (D.O.)*.
  me is the *indirect object (I.O.)*.

FORM

● *verb* + *direct object* + **to** or **for** + *indirect object*:

	D.O.		I.O.
Give	the money	to	him.
Buy	a present	for	your mother.

  a) Some common verbs taking **to**: **bring**, **give**, **lend**, **pay**, **promise**, **send**, **show**, **take**, **tell**.

  b) Some common verbs taking **for**: **buy**, **find**, **get**, **make**.

● *verb* + *indirect object* without **to** or **for** + *direct object*:

	I.O.	D.O.
Give	him	the money.
Buy	your mother	a present.

*   Note that it is not possible to use the second form when the direct object is a pronoun (**me**, **her**, **him**, **it**, etc). The longer construction must be used:
  Give it to John. (NOT ~~Give John it.~~)

131a Rewrite these sentences without using **to** or **for**:

1   Give this food to your parents.
     Give your parents this food.
2   Get an ashtray for me, please.
     Get me an ashtray, please.
3   Have you sent a postcard to your family?
4   Did you pay the money to him?
5   Would you find a seat for my mother, please?
6   I'll get some money for you.
7   Did you tell the news to your parents?
8   I'm buying a ticket for Jenny, too.
9   Show your painting to Mr Anderson.
10   Would you take this note to your parents?

131b Rewrite these sentences in the correct order:

11   to my parents / I / it / took
     I took it to my parents.
12   they / any money / me / didn't give
     They didn't give me any money.
13   to all / she / the car / her friends / showed
14   the students / the news / gave / I
15   did / my pen / lend / you / him?
16   bought / some flowers / my / I / parents / for
17   why / some cigarettes / didn't / me / bring / you?
18   some grapes and some flowers / took / Janice / we
19   his / showed / injured / me / hand / he
20   some vegetables from the garden / gave / our neighbours / we / to

132 ★★
Order of adverbs

- An *adverb* describes **how**, **where**, or **when** an action is done:
  a) *She hit him **gently**.*

- The adverb can be one word (e.g. **gently**) or a group of words – also called an *adverbial phrase*:
  b) *She hit him **with all her strength.***

- Both the adverb and the adverbial phrase in these two sentences answer the question *How did she hit him?*
  Answer: (a) gently (b) with all her strength.

- Adverbs that answer the question **how**? are *adverbs of manner*.

- Adverbs that answer the question **where**? are *adverbs of place*.
  *They work **here**.*
  *I saw them **at the end of the street**.*

● Adverbs that answer the question **when**? are *adverbs of time*.
  *He left **yesterday**.*
  *I saw him **at four o'clock**.*

● Order of adverbs:
  a) Adverbs of manner, place and time usually follow the direct object.
     I took the money **quietly**.
  b) If there is no direct object, the adverbs usually follow the verb:
     We left **at ten o'clock**.
  c) If there is more than one adverb, they are usually written:
     1 *manner*   2 *place*   3 *time*

	manner	*place*	*time*
I worked	hard	at the office	today.
I worked hard at the office today.			
They ran	quickly	into the house.	
They ran quickly into the house.			
We went		into the garden	at three o'clock.
We went into the garden at three o'clock.			
They played	noisily		all afternoon.
They played noisily all afternoon.			

NOTES

⇨ exercises 133 and 134 for adverbs of frequency (**always**, **usually**, **sometimes**, etc).

*   Adverbs of *time* and *place* are sometimes found at the beginning of sentences. (This emphasizes the importance of the time or place.)
    ***Yesterday** we had a really good time.*
    ***In Paris**, we stayed in hotels all the time.*

Rewrite these sentences in the correct order:

1   We had / at the party / a good time / yesterday.
    We had a good time at the party yesterday.
2   She played / last week / at the stadium / very well.
    She played very well at the stadium last week.
3   The children / in the garden / quietly / played / this afternoon.
4   He drove / through the town / very quickly.
5   He sat / all through the afternoon / in his chair / quietly.
6   They waited / in the rain / for two or three hours / patiently.
7   The plane / for about thirty minutes / slowly / flew / around Heathrow Airport.
8   We searched / thoroughly / the field / for several hours.
9   We worked / on Sunday / in the studio / hard.
10 I walked / after getting the news / slowly / to the end of the road.

11 He was sitting / on the edge of the bed / when I saw him / painfully.
12 They were arguing / in the kitchen / when I left / furiously.
13 The dog / up the stairs / slowly / climbed.
14 He talked / for several hours / loudly and confidently.
15 She was walking / around the hospital ward / slowly / when I visited her.

133 ★★
Frequency adverbs with the Present Simple

FORM

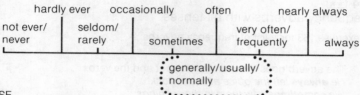

USE

● The adverb goes between the subject and the verb:
  I **often** see them.
  We **rarely** talk to them.
  I **seldom** go out in the evenings.

● **occasionally**, **sometimes**, **often**, **frequently**, and **normally** can also be at the beginning or end of a clause:
  I see them **occasionally**.
  Sometimes we talk to each other.
  Normally I go out in the evenings.

* Note that **always** is sometimes used with *present continuous* to express annoyance. **always** goes between the auxiliary verb and the main verb:
  Roger's **always** borrowing my things without asking!
  Peter's **always** complaining about his job!

Choose the correct word and write it in its proper place in these sentences:

1 I see them nowadays – the last time we met was ten years ago. (never / often / always)
  I never see them nowadays – the last time we met was ten years ago.
2 You're lucky: we have ice cream, but we've got some today. (hardly ever / normally / nearly always)
3 Peter's playing football instead of doing his homework. (seldom / hardly ever / always)
4 We go out now – we can't afford it. (hardly ever / sometimes / frequently)
5 I don't finish work before eleven o'clock, so I see the children before they go to bed. (always / never / usually)

6   I sit here when I come to the park – it's my favourite place. (hardly ever / occasionally / always)

7   She comes here nowadays – I don't think she likes me. (seldom / frequently / nearly always)

8   We don't go there every week, but we see them quite. (seldom / often / occasionally)

9   We see them, at least once a week. (frequently / occasionally / always)

10   I watch horror movies – I don't like them. (frequently / nearly always / hardly ever)

134 ★★
Frequency adverbs with all tenses

⇨ exercise 133 for a list of frequency adverbs.

● The adverb goes between the subject and the verb:
He **always** left the office at five o'clock.
We **sometimes** saw them in the evenings.
I **often** have an egg for breakfast.

● If the tense uses an auxiliary verb (**will**, **have**, **be**, or **do**), the adverb comes after the auxiliary, but before the infinitive or participle.
I'll **never** forget him.
I've **frequently** seen him in here.
I don't **always** agree with him.
Do you **often** come here?

● **occasionally**, **sometimes**, **often**, **frequently**, **normally** and **generally** can follow the verb or the verb + direct object. They can also be at the beginning or end of a clause:
I've seen him **frequently** in here.
I've seen him in here **frequently**.
Frequently, I've seen him in here.

Write the word given in the correct place in these sentences. Sometimes there is more than one answer. Choose the most likely one:

1   They got to the office on time. (never)
     They never got to the office on time.

2   I've seen them in the park. (sometimes)
     I've sometimes seen them in the park.
     I've seen them sometimes in the park.

3   I talked to them. (occasionally)

4   I phoned him at the office. (occasionally)

5   We'll see them again. (never)

6   I had written to them about their children. (frequently)

7   Do you watch this programme? (often)

8   I've been in a plane. (never)

9   She asked how you were. (often)

10   I've complained, but it didn't change anything. (frequently)
11   Don't you hear from your brother now? (ever)
12   I'll remember what he said. (always)
13   I've seen him in the supermarket. (occasionally)
14   We agreed that we would meet again. (never)
15   I've spoken to them. (hardly ever)
16   We saw them in the evenings. (seldom)
17   We've sent each other cards at Christmas. (always)
18   Those children are playing football in the street. (always)
19   They've been waiting when I come home from work. (often)
20   He's been working when I've seen him. (always)

135 ★★
Order of adjectives

There is a general order for adjectives:

number	general	size	shape	age	colour	pattern	material	nationality	adjectival noun	noun
A/An Some The Four	nice	large	square	old new	green	striped	woollen wooden metal	English Spanish French	kitchen garden	towel(s) table(s) chair(s)

For reasons of style, three or four adjectives are usually the maximum to be grouped together. When this happens, they generally follow the order in the box:

A large old wooden table.
Four green metal garden chairs.

Write these sentences in the correct order:

1   We bought some glasses German old lovely.
     We bought some lovely old German glasses.
2   Have you seen his sports Italian car new nice?
3   He lived in a wooden old hut dirty.
4   She was wearing a beautiful shirt silk black-and-white.
5   It's just custom strange another country old.
6   We stood under statue an wooden old enormous.
7   They gave him clock a silver beautiful.
8   I bought tablecloth a large striped red-and-white.
9   It was old lovely scarf a woollen green.
10 They sent him plates blue-and-white china expensive very some.

136a ☒
Link words: **and**, **but**, **so**, **then**, **before**, **after**, **because**

Write one of the above words in the correct place in these sentences. Use each word for two sentences. Where two answers are possible, choose the more likely one:

1   I got out of the car . . . . walked into the house.
     I got out of the car and walked into the house.
2   The weather was lovely, ... we stayed in the garden.
3   . . . . we went to bed I locked all the doors.
4   The little boy was wet and cold, ... he wasn't hurt.
5   We turned off the lights and . . . . left the room.
6   I had a bath . . . . we played football.
7   I sat in the kitchen . . . . read a book.
8   She worked hard, ... failed all her exams.
9   I do some exercises . . . . I go to work in the morning.
10   They took me to hospital . . . . the crash.
11   We had no money . . . . the banks were closed.
12   We paid our hotel bill and . . . . left.
13   I had to walk to work . . . . the car wouldn't start.
14   It was very cold, ... we didn't go out.

136b ☒☒
Link words: **although**, **however**, **though**, **in spite of**, **whereas**

Rewrite the sentences using the words given. You may need to change some words (and be careful with the punctuation). Where two answers are possible, choose the more likely one:

1   He seemed a friendly person – but I didn't like him. (although)
     Although he seemed a friendly person, I didn't like him.
2   My car wouldn't start. Jenny's started immediately. (whereas)
     My car wouldn't start, whereas Jenny's started immediately.
3   Jo never helped with the housework. Pat did. (whereas)
4   He lived in Germany for ten years – but he never learned German. (in spite of)
5   We sometimes stayed out late. We always got home before twelve. (though)
6   He didn't like sport: he didn't mind watching the football. (however)
7   I was very hungry. I had eaten an hour earlier. (in spite of)
8   The flat was comfortable. It was very expensive. (although)
9   My parents were angry. They soon forgave me. (though)
10   The old house was near the sea. The new one is in the middle of the town. (whereas)

Questions and answers

137 ☒
Making questions

- Questions are formed for all tenses except *present simple* and *past simple* by changing the position of the auxiliary verb (**am**, **was**, **will**, etc) and the subject (**I**, **you**, **she**, **he**, etc):

  You're going ⟶ ***Are you** going?*

  He has gone ⟶ ***Has he** gone?*

- Questions are formed for the *present simple* and *past simple* by using **do**, **does**, or **did**:

  They work here. ⟶ *Do they work here?*
  She lived here. ⟶ *Did she live here?*

⇨ exercise 26 and 34 for *present simple* and *past simple*.

Make questions from these statements:

1 She likes travelling.	10 They came today.
Does she like travelling?	11 She drives to work.
2 They're working.	12 He left this morning.
Are they working?	13 He was writing a letter.
3 He was playing tennis.	14 They watched television.
4 She went to school today.	15 She's at home.
5 They live here.	16 They went home.
6 She's eating at the moment.	17 She likes horror films.
7 They drove to the station.	18 He's walking home.
8 She's reading.	19 They were eating ice cream.
9 He had breakfast early.	20 They gave him the money.

138 ☒
wh questions

- **wh** words are **who**, **why**, **when**, **where**, **what**, and **how**. They are placed in front of the question:

  Are you going?

  ⟶ ***When** are you going?*

  ⟶ ***Where** are you going?*

  ⟶ ***What** time are you going?* etc.

Make ten questions from the box below, and give the answers:

Example:
Why did they leave?
Because they wanted to catch the train.

Who	
Why	are you going?
When	did they leave?
Where	is she talking to?
What	did they come here?
What time	are you looking at?
How	did it cost?
How much	

139 ★★
who as subject and object

What is the difference between
a) *Who saw you?* and b) *Who did you see?*

● In sentence (a), **who** is the subject of the sentence:
   s   v   o   s   v   o
   Someone saw you. Who saw you?

● In sentence (b), **who** is the object of the sentence:
   s   v   o   o   aux s   v
   You saw someone. Who did   you see?

NOTES

⇨ exercise 130 for subject and object.

* **whom** can be used as the object of the sentence:
   ***Whom** did you see?*
   but **whom** is not used very often now.

* **what** can also be the subject of a sentence:
   ***What** happened? **What** fell off the roof?*

Make **who** questions from these sentences:

1   You were talking to someone. Who . . . .
   Who were you talking to?
2   Someone was talking to you. Who . . . .
   Who was talking to you?
3   Someone telephoned me. Who . . . .
4   They wanted to see someone. Who . . . .
5   Someone sold you the car. Who . . . .
6   Someone gave you this money. Who . . . .

7   You told someone about the contract. Who . . . .
8   They have invited some people to the party. Who . . . .
9   They were arguing with someone. Who . . . .
10   Someone complained to the manager. Who . . . .
11   Someone wrote a letter to the school. Who . . . .
12   You didn't like somebody. Who . . . .
13   Someone opened the window. Who . . . .
14   She asked someone to help. Who . . . .
15   Someone wasn't at the meeting. Who . . . .

140 ★★
Tag questions

FORM

● A *tag question* is formed by auxiliary + subject (e.g. **did she? aren't they? have you?**)

● Positive sentences are generally followed by a negative tag question:
   *They went home, **didn't they**?*
   *It's hot, **isn't it**?*

● Negative sentences are generally followed by a positive tag question:
   *He's not waiting for us, **is he**?*
   *They didn't go home, **did they**?*

★ *Note the irregular form of* **I am** *when it is a negative tag question:*
   *I'm going with you, **aren't I**?*

USE

● *Tag questions* are often used to open conversations:
   It's a lovely day, isn't it?
   It's not very warm here, is it?

● They are used when we are expecting the person being questioned to agree with us:
   You're coming too, aren't you?
   They're not staying much longer, are they?

Rewrite these statements with *tag questions*:

1   It's cold.
     It's cold, isn't it?
2   He isn't very friendly.
     He isn't very friendly, is he?
3   You don't like eggs.
4   I'm staying too.
5   They're policemen.
6   She didn't arrive yesterday.
7   This shop's very expensive.
8   She's gone home.

9   This water's hot.
10   They're not coming this afternoon.
11   You haven't met my sister Jean.
12   He wasn't waiting at home for me.
13   She didn't like Pat when she met her.
14   They're going to write to us after they move.
15   He's got no money at the moment.
16   You liked some of the music you heard today.
17   You've nearly finished your book.
18   You're always forgetting your keys.
19   They've nearly finished the new school.
20   She's not very happy in her new job.

141 ⭐⭐
Agreeing with tag questions

- The short answer to a positive statement / negative tag is:
  Q: *He's leaving soon, isn't he?*
  A: *Yes, he is. / No, he isn't.*

- The short answer to a negative statement / positive tag is also:
  Q: *He isn't leaving today, is he?*
  A: *Yes, he is. / No, he isn't.*
  But here, *No, he isn't* is used to *agree* with the negative statement. (It is not possible to say *Yes, he isn't.*)

⇨ exercise 142 for the form of different short answers.

Write the correct short answers to agree with these questions:

1   'You're not angry, are you?'
      'No, I'm not.'
2   'They're staying in a hotel, aren't they?'
      'Yes, they are.'
3   'You said goodbye, didn't you?'
4   'She hasn't had a cup of tea, has she?'
5   'They didn't invite John, did they?'
6   'You haven't brought your car, have you?'
7   'She's seen this film already, hasn't she?'
8   'Mary isn't ill, is she?'
9   'You've heard about the meeting, haven't you?'
10   'Peter's not there already, is he?'

142 ⭐⭐
Short answers: check

- Short answers use the auxiliary, and not the main verb. The answer to:
  Did he say that? is
  Yes, he did. (NOT ~~Yes, he said.~~)

FORM

Yes/no + *subject* + *auxiliary verb* (*positive* or *negative*):

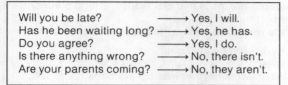

Will you be late?	⟶	Yes, I will.
Has he been waiting long?	⟶	Yes, he has.
Do you agree?	⟶	Yes, I do.
Is there anything wrong?	⟶	No, there isn't.
Are your parents coming?	⟶	No, they aren't.

NOTES
*   Agreement to a negative question is indicated by using **No** and repeating the negative:
    Isn't he coming? ⟶ *No, he isn't.* (⇨ exercise 141)

⇨ exercises 31 and 40 for other exercises on short answers.

Write short answers for these questions, using the *positive* or *negative* as given:

1	'You won't be late today, will you?'	*'No, I won't.'*
2	'Did they leave early this morning?'	*'Yes, they did.'*
3	'Have you checked the car?'	'Yes, ...'
4	'Is there any petrol in it?'	'Yes, ...'
5	'Have you been working here very long?'	'Yes, ...'
6	'Have you finished your homework yet?'	'No, ...'
7	'Were they angry about what you said?'	'No, ...'
8	'Are they going to see us before they leave?'	'No, ...'
9	'Is he washing the dishes?'	'Yes, ...'
10	'Will you be seeing Jayne tomorrow?'	'No, ...'
11	'Haven't they told you what to do?'	'No, ...'
12	'He isn't going to apologize, is he?'	'No, ...'
13	'They haven't given you any money, have they?'	'No, ...'
14	'Hadn't she told you about Mrs Jameson?'	'No, ...'
15	'This dress is very expensive, isn't it?'	'Yes, ...'
16	'You don't like his parents, do you?'	'No, ...'
17	'He said you were wrong, didn't he?'	'Yes, ...'
18	'You won't forget the meeting, will you?'	'No, ...'
19	'It's Saturday today, isn't it?'	'Yes, ...'
20	'Didn't I talk to you about this yesterday?'	'No, ...'

143 ★★

Embedded questions

● Embedded questions are those that are 'hidden' in long questions:
  Where's the bank? (normal question)
  *Could you tell me **where the bank is?*** (embedded question)

● There are two types of embedded question:
  a) in reported speech:
     She asked me where the airport was. (⇨ exercises 122 to 124)
  b) in polite question forms, when the direct question is thought to be
     a little rude, and a longer question form is used:
     Could you tell me what time it is, please?
     Do you think this train is going to be late?

FORM

● The position of subject and auxiliary verb in the normal question form
  is reversed:

  *Where **has she** gone?* ⟶ *where **she has** gone.*

● A polite question form is now put in front of this new structure:
  Could you tell me where she has gone?

● The most commonly used polite question forms are:

Could you tell me Do you know Do you think you could tell me	if whether where how why	something	happened? has happened? will happen? is going to happen? etc

Do you think	(that) something	happened? will happen? etc

* Remember you must say: *Could you tell me where she has gone?*
  (NOT ~~Could you tell me where has she gone?~~)

Write these sentences in full, using the words given:

1 Could you tell me / When does the train leave?
  Could you tell me when the train leaves?
2 Do you think that / Is it going to rain today?
  Do you think that it's going to rain today?
3 Do you know if / Has everybody left already?
4 Do you think you could tell me / What time is it, please?
5 Do you know / Why is there nobody here?

6   Could you tell me / Why did you leave so early?
7   Do you know if / Is the meeting cancelled?
8   Do you think / Will there be a lot of people at the party?
9   Could you tell me / What time does this shop close?
10   Do you know / How much is this?
11   Do you think you could tell me / When does the plane from Paris
     arrive?
12   Do you think / Will there be another train tonight?
13   Could you tell me / When will you be finished?
14   Do you know / How long will we have to wait?
15   Do you think you could tell me / Where's the post office?

144 ★★
think, hope, expect, suppose

● These verbs are often used as answers to embedded questions (and
  to ordinary questions, too):

'Do you think the train will arrive soon?'

'Yes, I think so.'
(NOT *'Yes, I think.'*)

'I hope so.'

'I expect so.'

FORM

> *Positive:* I think / hope / expect / suppose so.
> *Negative:* I don't think / expect / suppose so.
> I hope not / I suppose not.

NOTES

★   It is possible to say **I think not** (which is a little formal). **I expect not** is
     quite unusual.

★   These constructions can also be used with the third person (**he**, **she**,
     they):
     She hopes so.
     They don't think so.
     although the first person (**I/we**) is more commonly heard.

Write the short answers according to the words given:

1 'Do you think we'll get there before dark?' (Yes / think)
  'Yes, I think so.'
2 'Will there be something to eat when we get there?' (No / suppose)
  'No, I don't suppose so.'
3 'Will the game start at three?' (Yes / expect)
4 'Do you think we'll lose the election?' (No / suppose)
5 'Do you think they'll be delayed?' (No / hope)
6 'Do you think it'll rain tomorrow?' (No / think)
7 'Are the tickets going to be expensive?' (No / hope)
8 'Will they give Sheila a job?' (Yes / expect)
9 'Do you think it'll be a good party?' (Yes / think)
10 'Are they going to bring the sandwiches?' (Yes / suppose)

Relative clauses

145 ★★★
Relative clauses with **who** and **that**

- Look at this sentence:
  The man gave me some money.

- If we want to describe the man, we can use an adjective (**old**, **thin**, **young**, etc):
  The old man gave me some money.

- However, sometimes the information we want to give is more complicated.
  The old man met me at the airport. He gave me some money.

- The two sentences can be combined, to show **which** old man gave me the money:
  The old man who met me at the airport gave me some money.
  who met me at the airport is a *clause* (a mini-sentence in the larger sentence). It is called a *relative clause* because it relates to (= connects with) a noun in the larger sentence.

FORM

- *Relative clauses* are often indicated by **who** (for people) and **that** (for things). The *relative clause* is placed immediately after the noun which it describes.

  I was talking to a person who had worked with my father.

  The machine that I wanted to buy was too expensive.

NOTES

*   **that** is sometimes used for people, and **which** for things
  (⇨ exercise 150).

*   **who** or **that** replaces the pronoun: *This is the man who I met in Paris.*
  (NOT *This is the man **who** I met **him** in Paris.*)

Join each pair of sentences together to make one sentence,
using **who** or **that**. Write the second sentence as a relative clause:

1   This is the man. I met him in Paris.
     This is the man who I met in Paris.
2   I wanted the painting. You bought it.
     I wanted the painting that you bought.
3   This is the chair. My parents gave it to me.
4   She's the woman. She telephoned the police.
5   He's the person. He wanted to buy your house.
6   We threw out the computer. It never worked properly.
7   This is the lion. It's been ill recently.
8   The man was badly injured. He was driving the car.
9   The children broke my window. They live in the next street.
10   That's the woman. I was telling you about her.

146 ★★★
Subject and object relative clauses

●   The noun which is being described by a clause can be either the
subject or object of the relative clause:
The man who normally works here is ill.
Main sentence: *The man is ill.*
Clause: *who normally works here.*
                 = ***he** normally works here.*
he is the subject, so this is a *subject relative clause.*

The man who you saw yesterday is ill.
Main sentence: *The man is ill.*
Clause: *who you saw yesterday.*
           = *you saw **him** yesterday.*
him is the object, so this is an *object relative clause.*

Write these sentences in your notebook and underline the relative clauses.
Write S or O to indicate whether it is a subject or object clause:

1   The woman <u>who I spoke to</u> wasn't very polite. *O*
2   The machine <u>that worked better than the others</u> cost the least. *S*
3   I wouldn't stay in a hotel that refused to accept children.
4   I don't understand people who hate animals.
5   The stereo that I bought last week doesn't work properly.
6   The television that they have designed is going to be very expensive.

7   That man who complained is always making trouble.
8   The woman who gave us all this money is not very rich.
9   I admire people who can speak more than one language.
10   The assistant who you complained about has been moved.

147 ⟨★★★⟩

Contact clauses (relative clauses without **who**, **that** or **which**)

● If a clause is an *object relative clause* and it is defining (⟹ exercise
   149), **who**, **that**, or **which** is not necessary:
   a) *She's the person **who** I met at the conference.*
      ⟶ *She's the person I met at the conference.*
   b) *Have you seen the dress **that** I've just bought?*
      ⟶ *Have you seen the dress I've just bought?*

● Note that this is not possible with *subject relative clauses*:
   The man who was feeling ill left early.
   (NOT ~~The man was feeling ill left early.~~)

Express each pair of sentences as one, without using **who**, **that**, or **which**.
Think carefully about the word order:

1   I shouted at a man. He didn't come back again.
     The man I shouted at didn't come back again.
2   I dropped a television. It never worked again.
     The television I dropped never worked again.
3   I hired a machine. It was broken.
4   She bought some clothes. They were beautiful.
5   They built a wall. It fell down after three weeks.
6   I asked a policeman. He wasn't very helpful.
7   We bought a car. I didn't really like it.
8   I borrowed some money from Janice. I lost it.
9   They sent a new teacher. I really liked her.
10   I sacked a sales assistant. I had a terrible argument with him.

148 ⟨★★⟩
whose

● **whose** is used to indicate possession:
   There's the man. His wallet was stolen.
   ⟶ *There's the man whose wallet was stolen.*

*   Note the difference between **whose** and **who's**: **who's** is never used
     to indicate possession, but is a contraction of **who is** or **who has**:
     She's the one who's lending us the money. (who's lending = who is
     lending)

Express each pair of sentences as one, using **whose** or **who's**:

1   There's the lady. Her dog was killed.
     There's the lady whose dog was killed.

2   That's the man. He's going to buy the company.
    That's the man who's going to buy the company.
3   He's the person. His car was stolen.
4   She's the new doctor. She's coming to the hospital next month.
5   She's the journalist. Her article was on the front page of *The Times*.
6   They're the people. Their shop burned down last week.
7   That's the sales director. He's leaving in March.
8   That's the student. Her parents complained about the school.
9   She's the singer. She's just signed a contract with a recording
    company.
10 He's the person. He's going to be promoted.
11 I'm the one. My flat was broken into.
12 She's the person. She's working for the film studios.
13 That's the architect. She's just won a prize for design.
14 That's the boy. He's just got a place at university.
15 I'm the person. You stayed in my flat.

149 ★★
Defining and non-defining relative clauses: recognition

- There are two types of relative clause: *defining* and *non-defining*.

- *Defining clauses* are more common than non-defining clauses:
  'I saw that man again.'
  'Which man?'
  'The man who wants to buy my house.'
  who wants to buy my house is an example of a *defining clause*: it
  defines (= explains) exactly who or what is being discussed. It can
  also be used in a longer sentence:
  The man who wants to buy my house is coming to see me.
  I saw the man who wants to buy my house again.

- *Non-defining* clauses give information about the subject being
  discussed, but it is not essential information:
  A man, who said he knew my father, asked me for money.
  who said he knew my father is an interesting fact but it is extra rather
  than essential information. Non-defining clauses are indicated by the
  use of commas before and after the clause.

NOTES

*   *Non-defining clauses* are used in writing but are not used frequently
    in conversation, where two short sentences can be enough:
    I'm going to see Sheila, who I told you about yesterday.
    I'm going to see Sheila. I told you about her yesterday.

*   The difference between defining (D) and non-defining (ND) clauses is
    important because:
    a) they can change the meaning of a sentence:
       D: *I have two sisters who are living in New York at the moment.*
       ND: *I have two sisters, who are living in New York at the moment.*

In the non-defining sentence the person has only two sisters.
In the defining sentence the person has two sisters in New
York, and may have more sisters somewhere else.

b) Different relative pronouns (**who**, **that**, **which**, etc) are used for
defining and non-defining clauses (⇨ exercise 150).

Copy these sentences into your notebook, and write D or ND to indicate
whether the clause is *defining* or *non-defining*:

1   The bus, which arrived late, was full. *ND*
2   The bus which they sent didn't have enough seats. *D*
3   The house which we wanted to buy was too expensive.
4   The house, which we wanted to buy, was too expensive.
5   I have two brothers who are working as architects at the moment.
6   I have two brothers, who are working as architects at the moment.
7   I never met the doctor, who lived next door for five years.
8   Did I ever tell you about my uncle, who left school when he was 15?
9   I didn't agree with the man who said we should cancel the trip.
10 She's one of those people who will argue about anything.

150 ★★
Relative pronouns in defining and non-defining clauses

who, **that**, or **which**?

Defining:

	person	thing
Subject	who (or that)	that (or which)
Object	– (or that)	– (or that)

Non-defining:

	person	thing
Subject	,who . . . ,	, which . . . ,
Object	,who (or whom) . . . ,	, which . . . ,

NOTES

*   Words in brackets ( ) are possible alternatives to the words given, but
    are less common.

*   **whom** is used only in formal English.

*   *Object relative clauses* do not normally need **who** or **that** (⇨ exercise
    147).

Write **who**, **that**, **which**, or nothing to complete these sentences. The boxes
above will help you, but do not use the words in brackets:

1   Have you got the money . . . . I lent you yesterday?
    Have you got the money I lent you yesterday?

2 Peter, ... I had seen earlier, wasn't at the party.
Peter, who I had seen earlier, wasn't at the party.
3 This is the machine . . . . cost half a million pounds.
4 Mary, ... had been listening to the conversation, looked angry.
5 Have you read the book . . . . I gave you?
6 The house, ... they bought three months ago, looks lovely.
7 Mrs Jackson, ... had been very ill, died yesterday.
8 Is this the person . . . . stole your handbag?
9 The dog, ... had been very quiet, suddenly started barking.
10 I didn't receive the letters . . . . she sent me.
11 My mother, ... hadn't been expecting visitors, looked surprised.
12 The old man, ... had been talking to them earlier, knew that they were in the building.
13 The horse, ... had been injured by the flying stones, was very frightened.
14 We didn't like the secretary . . . . the agency sent.
15 I didn't find the money . . . . you said you'd left.

151 ★★★
which referring to whole sentences

● **which** in relative clauses generally refers to nouns:
He turned on the television, which looked new and expensive.
which here refers to **the television**.

● **which** can also refer to whole sentences:
He turned on the television. I thought this was rather surprising.
He turned on the television, which I thought was rather surprising.

NOTES

* **which** here refers to **the action of turning on the television**, not just to the television.

* **which** can be used like this only in *non-defining relative clauses* (⇨ exercise 149).

Express these pairs of sentences as one, using **which**. You will need to change some words:

1 I love the countryside. That is why I want to go and live there.
I love the countryside, which is why I want to go and live there.
2 They stayed for hours. I was very annoyed about this.
They stayed for hours, which I was very annoyed about.
3 He passed all his exams. This surprised us.
4 They forgot about my birthday. This was a bit disappointing.
5 The pilot showed us how to fly the plane. It was extremely interesting.
6 I couldn't get a flight to Malaga. This upset the children.
7 He was rude and aggressive. His behaviour made me very angry.
8 They said they couldn't pay for the car immediately. This made me a bit suspicious.

9   The policeman asked me for directions. This confused me a little.
10   The restaurant wouldn't accept cheques. I found this rather surprising.

152 ★★★

where, **when**, and **why** in relative clauses

● **where** and **when** can be used to introduce *defining* and *non-defining relative clauses*:
   We visited the town where I was born. (defining)
   I bought them at the supermarket, where I met Mrs Butler. (non-defining)
   I saw the film last year, when I was in Paris. (non-defining)
   I think that was the time when I lost all my money. (defining)

● Less often, **why** can also be used to introduce a defining clause: it usually follows **a reason** or **the reason**:
   There must be a reason why you said that.

Write **where**, **when**, or **why** to complete these sentences:

1   We visited the school .... my father taught.
     We visited the school where my father taught.
2   I met her last month, ... she came to our house.
     I met her last month, when she came to our house.
3   We all looked at the place .... the fire had started.
4   I met him in the café, ... he was working as a waiter.
5   Do you remember the time .... Adrian fell off his bicycle?
6   Did they tell you the reason .... they were late?
7   The cat sat on the wall, ... it had a good view of the birds.
8   I'm talking about the time .... they didn't have cars.
9   Last year I spent my holiday in Yugoslavia, ... I met Andy.
10   I couldn't understand the reason .... they were so rude.
11   I bought them last year, ... I was in France.
12   We went away in August, ... the children were on holiday from school.
13   I never liked the house .... my husband was born.
14   They arrived in the evening, at a time .... we were all out.
15   I listen to music late at night, ... the children have gone to bed.

Prepositions

Prepositions of place

153 ☒
at, in, on

● **at** is used for a place when the exact position is not very important:

*He was standing **at** the gate.* ●✕
*We were waiting **at** the station.* ●✕

● **on** is used when the place is seen as a line or surface:

*The cat sat **on** the table.* ──●
*There was a picture **on** the wall.*

● **in** is used when the place is seen as having volume or area:

*The dog was **in** the car.*
*My keys are **in** my bag.*

Write **at**, **in**, or **on** to complete these sentences. If two answers are possible, write the more likely one:

1   Peter's . . . . the kitchen.
    Peter's in the kitchen.
2   The money's . . . . the table.
    The money's on the table.
3   He was waiting . . . . the station.
    He was waiting at the station.
4   The milk's . . . . the fridge.
5   They sat . . . . the wall.
6   They made the film . . . . Shepperton Studios.
7   I saw them . . . . the station.
8   Mary's not here – she's . . . . the office.
9   They were sitting . . . . the floor.
10 The butter's . . . . the shelf . . . . the cupboard.
11 The money's . . . . my pocket.
12 They are all . . . . the garden.
13 The papers are . . . . my desk.
14 They are all . . . . the car.
15 He's not . . . . work today – he's . . . . home.

154 ⊠
Prepositions of movement

● **to**, **at**, or **away from** a place

to	at	(away) from

*She ran **to** the gate.*
*She stood **at** the gate.*
*She walked **away from** the gate.*

● **on**, **onto**, or **off** a line or surface (a wall, table, floor, etc)

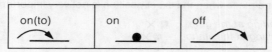

on(to)	on	off

*I put the money **onto** the table.*
*The money's **on** the table.*
*The money fell **off** the table.*

● **in**, **into**, or **out of** a box, car, or anything with volume

in(to)	in	out (of)

*The dog jumped **into** the car.*
*The dog's **in** the car.*
*Take the dog **out of** the car.*

Choose the correct words from the boxes to complete these sentences:

1   She was standing . . . . the front door.
     She was standing at the front door.
2   I put the matches . . . . the table.
3   She got . . . . the car and ran . . . . the station.
4   The baby's going to fall . . . . the table.
5   The bread's . . . . the cupboard.
6   I walked . . . . the church and waited . . . . the bus stop.
7   He was lying . . . . the floor.
8   She dived . . . . the sea.
9   They climbed . . . . the roof, and looked down at us.
10   We walked . . . . the end of the road.

155 ⭑⭑
Prepositions of position and movement

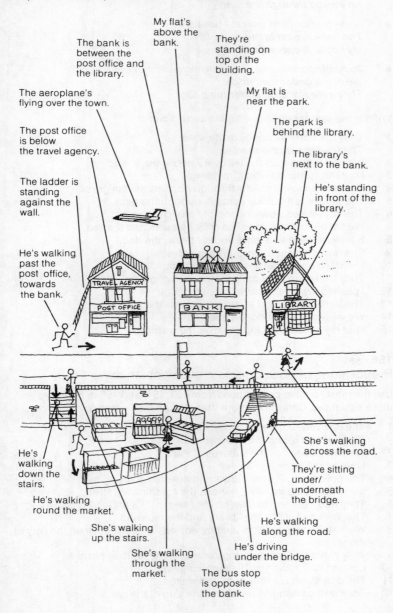

My flat's above the bank.

The bank is between the post office and the library.

They're standing on top of the building.

The aeroplane's flying over the town.

My flat is near the park.

The post office is below the travel agency.

The park is behind the library.

The library's next to the bank.

The ladder is standing against the wall.

He's standing in front of the library.

He's walking past the post office, towards the bank.

He's walking down the stairs.

She's walking across the road.

They're sitting under/ underneath the bridge.

He's walking round the market.

He's walking along the road.

She's walking up the stairs.

He's driving under the bridge.

She's walking through the market.

The bus stop is opposite the bank.

- Some prepositions indicate movement:
  *I ran **past** the school.*
  *He walked **through** the gate.*

- Some prepositions indicate position:
  *The bank is **next to** the post office.*
  *My house is **opposite** the school.*

- Some prepositions can indicate movement or position:
  *We drove **under** the bridge.*
  *They were standing **under** the bridge.*

Write these sentences, choosing the correct word:

1 They ran across / opposite the road.
   They ran across the road.
2 We had a picnic on the hill over / above the village.
3 I put the ladder against / up the wall.
4 The snake moved quietly through / across the tall grass.
5 The mouse ran quickly across / through the path.
6 The cat walked slowly on top of / along the wall.
7 We sat on top of / along the cliffs and watched the sea.
8 Someone pushed a letter under / below the door.
9 She drove between / through the gates.
10 I held the parcel behind / past my back.
11 They walked in front of / past the school gate.
12 I pushed my bike over / above the bridge.
13 The bank clerk stood against / towards the wall.
14 We waited down / under a tree.
15 I put my suitcase on top of / over the wardrobe.

156 ★★
Prepositions of position and movement: check

Use the most suitable prepositions from 153, 154, and 155 to complete these sentences. Sometimes more than one answer is possible:

1 The dog ran . . . . the tree five or six times.
   The dog ran round the tree five or six times.
2 We flew slowly . . . . the suburbs of Paris.
3 I moved the baby . . . . the fire.
4 The police ran . . . . the crowd and arrested a young man.
5 If you put some money . . . . here, the machine will start.
6 They had nowhere to stay, so they slept . . . . a bridge.
7 The town hall is . . . . the library and the museum.
8 We watched the soldiers as they walked . . . . our house on the way to the ship.
9 They ran out of the dressing-room . . . . the football pitch.
10 London is . . . . the south-east of England.
11 The dog stood . . . . the door and waited.
12 They walked hand-in-hand . . . . the side of the canal.

13 I didn't want my mother to see her present, so I held it . . . . my back.
14 The cat jumped . . . . my arms and ran away.
15 I threw the stone . . . . the sea.
16 The bottles fell . . . . the lorry and rolled . . . . the hill.
17 It was too dark to see, so he walked slowly, holding his arms . . . . him.
18 I put a chair . . . . the door to stop anyone coming in.
19 We crawled . . . . a hole in the fence.
20 What have you got . . . . your hand?
21 The cat was sitting . . . . the cupboard, looking down at me.
22 I was frightened. I could see him walking . . . . me, with a very angry
    look on his face.
23 I tied the string . . . . my waist.
24 If you are feeling sick, you should sit . . . . a chair and put your head
    . . . . your knees.
25 The cat jumped out of the tree . . . . the roof of my car.

157 ★★★
Prepositions used in idioms

● Prepositions are sometimes used idiomatically:

*I got the job **through** my uncle.*

*She's been promoted. She's got two hundred
people working **under** her now.*

Use these prepositions to complete the sentences:

in front of	against	below
behind	against	below
behind	between	above
past	on top of	above

1 He doesn't do much work in the house: in fact, he seems to think he's
   . . . . that sort of thing.
   He doesn't do much work in the house: in fact, he seems to think he's
   above that sort of thing.
2 It's a very good article. There's obviously a lot of research . . . . it.
3 I work for an organization which campaigns . . . . smoking.
4 It was very cold, about twenty degrees . . . . zero.
5 He tells me everything. There are no secrets . . . . us.

6   It was difficult to get the idea . . . . the board of directors, but they finally agreed.
7   The company is doing well; sales were . . . . average last month.
8   I think you should forget about your argument and put it all . . . . you.
9   They have a very good future . . . . them.
10   It's terrible: their wages are . . . . the national minimum.
11   We've never played . . . . a Swiss team before.
12   The work was difficult at first, but I soon got . . . . it.

158 ★★
Certain verbs with **to** or **at**

● Some verbs are followed by **to** or **at**, and some verbs do not use a preposition:
   Listen to me!
   Look at that!
   She **told** me the news.

Write **to**, **at** or nothing to complete these sentences:

1   I sent the parcel . . . . her yesterday.
   I sent the parcel to her yesterday.
2   Are you going to phone . . . . your parents now?
3   What did you say . . . . them?
4   The children were terrified when he shouted . . . . them.
5   What did you tell . . . . them?
6   I took the box out of my pocket and gave it . . . . her.
7   We explained the problem . . . . the attendant.
8   I don't know why they were laughing . . . . us.
9   She caught the ball and threw it gently back . . . . me.
10   They were arrested for throwing stones . . . . the police.

Prepositions of time

159 ★
at, in, on

● **at** a point in time:
   at four o'clock, **at** bedtime

● **on** a day or date:
   on Monday, **on** July 6th, **on** your birthday

● **in** a period of time:
   in the morning, **in** April, **in** the summer, **in** 1987

*   Note: **at** night, **at** Christmas, **at** Easter

*   **on** Monday, **in** the morning, **on** Monday morning

Write **at**, **in**, or **on** to complete these sentences.

1   I'll see you . . . . Monday.
     I'll see you on Monday.
2   I met him . . . . the holidays.
3   I'll pick you up . . . . eight o'clock.
4   I'm going home . . . . four.
5   They came to visit us . . . . my birthday.
6   I can work . . . . the morning, but I don't like working . . . . night.
7   Did you have a good time . . . . Christmas?
8   School finishes . . . . three o'clock . . . . Thursdays.
9   We arranged to meet . . . . seven . . . . the morning.
10   We had a party . . . . the last day of the course.

160 ★★
Prepositions of time

Use one of these words to complete the sentences below:

until	during	after	before
through	between	from	in

1   I waited . . . . nine o'clock and then went home.
     I waited until nine o'clock and then went home.
2   If you come . . . . seven, we'll catch the bus that leaves at 7.05.
3   Will you come and see me . . . . a week or two?
4   . . . . the children left, the house was very quiet.
5   . . . . the holidays, we played tennis and did a lot of swimming.
6   I can't remember when we left the cinema: I think it was . . . . ten and half-past ten.
7   I was ill . . . . January to March.
8   We worked all . . . . the holidays to finish painting the boat.

NOTES

⇨ exercise 44 for **for** and **since**.
⇨ exercise 132 for adverbs of time.

Phrasal verbs

- A phrasal verb is formed when a *preposition* (**up**, **down**, **in**, etc) or an *adverb* (**away**, **back**, etc) is added to a verb to produce a new verb with a different meaning:

  I **get up** at eight o'clock.

  We'll **pick** you **up** outside the station.

  The plane **took off** very quickly.

- The meaning of a phrasal verb can be similar to the original verb:

  The car **slowed down** and then stopped. (= similar meaning to **slow**)

  – or it can be completely different to the original:
  I'm going to **give up** smoking. (= different meaning to **give**)

- There are four main types of phrasal verb which are described in exercises 163 to 166.

161 ⋆
Some common phrasal verbs

wake up	look after	ring up
get up	sit down	get on
stand up	give up	

Choose the correct phrasal verbs from the list above to complete these sentences:

1   The children . . . . at eight o'clock to have breakfast.
     The children get up at eight o'clock to have breakfast.
2   '. . . .!' he said. 'This is not the time for sleeping!'
3   After the crash, my legs hurt: it was very difficult to . . . . .
4   '. . . . in that chair, please,' said the doctor.
5   The bus was moving too fast, and I couldn't . . . . it.
6   Mr and Mrs Smith are going to . . . . the children for an hour.
7   I'm going to . . . . smoking tomorrow.
8   I'm going to . . . . the station and ask about the trains.

162 ★★
More phrasal verbs

blow up	grow up	put off
break down	keep on	run out of
find out	let down	set off
get over	look out	tell off
go on	look up	turn down

Write the above verbs in the correct tenses to complete these sentences.
Use each verb once only:

1   We'll buy a smaller house when the children have . . . . and left home.
     We'll buy a smaller house when the children have grown up and left
     home.
2   'Sorry, we . . . . flour,' she said. 'We'll have some next week.'
3   The computer isn't working – it . . . . this morning.
4   I . . . . where he lived by checking in the local library.
5   It was no problem: we . . . . his number in the telephone book.
6   They . . . . working all through the night, and finished at nine this
     morning.
7   'I can't come today,' he said. 'We'll have to . . . . the meeting until next
     week.'
8   We must . . . . early on Sunday morning to avoid the traffic.
9   I was . . . . by the teacher because I hadn't done my homework.
10   He had a very painful illness, but he's . . . . it now.
11   'What's . . . . here? What are you doing?'
12   '. . . .!' she cried. 'He's got a gun!'
13   I . . . . their offer because they weren't going to pay me enough money.
14   He promised to be at the match, but he didn't come. He . . . . the whole
     team.
15   The car burned for a few minutes, then the petrol tank . . . . with a
     loud bang.

163 ★★★
Phrasal verbs that do not take an object

●   Some phrasal verbs do not take an object:
     *The plan **fell through**: we had to cancel the project.*

get by	pass away	sleep in
grow up	set off	take off

Put the above verbs into the correct sentences, using the right tense:

1   She had a terrible shock when her father . . . . .
     She had a terrible shock when her father passed away.

2   I didn't have to go to work that morning, so I decided to . . . . .
3   How do you . . . . with so little money?
4   The explorers . . . . in the morning, before it was too hot.
5   After the children . . . . and left, the house seemed empty.
6   What time does the plane . . . .?

164 ★★★
Separable phrasal verbs that take an object

● We can say:
*We **picked up** the children at three.* or
*We **picked** the children **up** at three.*

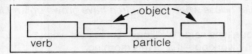

● The *direct object* can go:
a) *before* the particle (= preposition or adverb)
*We decided to **cut** the tree **down**.*
b) *after* the particle:
*We decided to **cut down** the tree.*

● If the object is a pronoun (**him**, **me**, **it**, etc) it goes *before* the particle:
*We decided to **cut** it **down**.*
(NOT ~~We cut down it.~~)

Write these sentences putting the verbs and objects in the correct order.
Where two answers are possible, write them both:

1   How do you / slow down / the machine?

How do you slow down the machine?
How do you slow the machine down?
2   The company decided to / give away / a hundred pounds.
3   I / turned on / the television.
4   It's a nice dress: would you like to / try on / it?
5   The government wants to / close down / the factory.
6   It's too wet for football. I think we'll have to / call off / it.
7   I couldn't accept his offer so I / turned down / him.
8   The baby's fallen over: would you / pick up / her?

165 ★★★
Phrasal verbs that take an object but do not separate

● This type of verb is a unit that is not split by the object:
  *How are we going to **get round** this problem?*
  (NOT *How are we going to get this problem round?*)

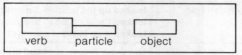

The object must follow the particle.

Write these sentences putting the verbs and objects in the correct order:

1 She looks like her mother: don't you think she / her / after / takes?
  She looks like her mother: don't you think she takes after her?
2 His wife died. He / her death / over / got / never.
3 She has a small pension. She / off / lives / that.
4 When Pat and John visited their parents / the children / after / I / looked.
5 I'm sorry, I forgot your sunglasses: you'll have to / them / without/ do.
6 I saw Peter today. He / you / after / asked.

166 ★★★
Phrasal verbs with two particles

● This type of phrasal verb is a unit that does not split:
  *'I'm not going to **put up with** this,' he said.*

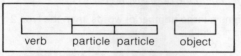

The object follows the second particle.

run out of	keep on at	look down on
come up with	go back on	

Choose one of the above verbs to complete each sentence below:

1 I'm afraid we've . . . . milk.
2 He doesn't like them: I think he . . . . people who haven't got any
  money.
3 You can trust her: she never . . . . her promises.
4 He . . . . me until I agreed to go to the party with him.
5 She . . . . an idea that solved the problem.

167 ★★★
Summary of phrasal verbs

	Type	Example
1	verb takes no object	The plane **takes off** at ten.
2	verb takes object: verb can split	I **looked up** the word in the dictionary. I **looked** the word **up** in the dictionary. I **looked** it **up** in the dictionary.
3	verb takes object: verb cannot split	I saw John today: he **asked after** you.
4	verb has two particles: does not split	We've **run out of** bread.

NOTES

* Many verbs are followed by prepositions, but this does not mean that they are phrasal verbs. A phrasal verb has a meaning as a unit. The following are verbs + prepositions:
  *What do you **think about** the idea?*
  ***Look at** these clothes!*
  With verbs + prepositions the direct object always follows the preposition, but the preposition does not have to come immediately after the verb:
  *We **looked** carefully **at** all the clothes.*
  *He **thought** for some minutes, and with much regret, **about** his parents.*

* Phrasal verbs can sometimes be type 1, or type 2, depending on their meaning:
  *'Goodbye!' she said, and **hung up**.* (= put the phone down). (type 1)
  *I **hung** my coat **up** behind the door.* (type 2)

* If the object contains a large number of words, then the type 2 phrasal verb does not split:

  *Have you **looked up**ᵒ the word we were talking about this morning?*

168 ★★★
Deducing phrasal verbs from context

● Sometimes the meaning of phrasal verbs can be understood from the context of the sentence:
  *It will hurt at first, but the pain will soon **wear off**.*
  It is not difficult to guess that **wear off** means 'to get less and less until it disappears'.

168a Read this passage and decide the meanings of the missing verbs:

'. . . I was having a terrible time until recently. About a month ago I was feeling really fed up with my job: nothing was going right, and I hated going to work. My boss was always (1) . . . . me – ordering me around and telling me I hadn't done things properly: I just couldn't (2) . . . . it any longer. I'd even (3) . . . . the work itself: I used to like it, but I wasn't getting any enjoyment out of it any more. Then one day the boss came in and accused me of (4) . . . . late for work all the time. I couldn't believe it! I'd only been late once that month and he was always (5) . . . . halfway through the morning. I asked him where he'd (6) . . . . this information and he said that one of the secretaries had told him. I said that it just wasn't true and that she must be (7) . . . . me because she didn't like me. Anyway I got really annoyed and in the end just (8) . . . ., slamming the door behind me. I (9) . . . . my resignation and left that day.

Well, fortunately things have (10) . . . . since then. I (11) . . . . evening classes in photography after leaving my job and met a solicitor there. She (12) . . . . the idea that I should go and work in her office, so I did! It's much more interesting than the last job so, as it happened, things (13) . . . . well in the end!

168b Here is a list of verbs with their definitions. Choose the correct verbs and write them in the correct tenses to complete the passage above:

get at – continually annoy Answer: *(1) getting at* come up with – suggest work out – result, eventually develop get hold of – obtain storm out – leave angrily pick on – choose for unpleasant treatment	hand in – give (resignation, or an official form) to an office put up with – tolerate pick up – improve go off – not like any more take up – start turn up – arrive drift in (*colloquial*) – arrive lazily

Index

Note that all numbers in this index are page numbers.